JOURNAL THERAPY

~for~

OVERCOMING BURNOUT

366 Prompts for Renewal and Stress Management

~

KATHLEEN ADAMS, LPC

WITH LINDA BARNES, LEIA FRANCISCO, CAROLYN KOEHNLINE,
DEBORAH ROSS, AND NANCY SCHERLONG

STERLING
New York

STERLING
New York

An Imprint of Sterling Publishing Co., Inc.

ISBN 978-1-4549-4358-7

Distributed in Canada by Sterling Publishing Co., Inc.
c/o Canadian Manda Group, 664 Annette Street
Toronto, Ontario M6S 2C8, Canada
Distributed in the United Kingdom by GMC Distribution Services
Castle Place, 166 High Street, Lewes, East Sussex BN7 1XU, England
Distributed in Australia by NewSouth Books
University of New South Wales, Sydney, NSW 2052, Australia

For information about custom editions, special sales, and premium and corporate
purchases, please contact Sterling Special Sales at 800-805-5489 or specialsales@
sterlingpublishing.com.

Manufactured in Canada

2 4 6 8 10 9 7 5 3 1

sterlingpublishing.com

Interior design by Gina Bonanno
Cover design by Elizabeth Mihalste Lindy

Image Credits:
Getty Images: stevegraham/Digital Vion Vectors: weeks 21–24, 45–48
Offset/Shutterstock.com: fstop images: cover, i

Shutterstock.com: alexcoolok: weeks 17–20, 41–44; Ann in the uk: weeks 9–12, 33–36;
Makhnach_S: weeks 1–4; Midorie: weeks 5–8, 29–35, 53; OK-SANA: weeks 25–28, 49–52;
rvika: weeks 13–16, 37–40

INTRODUCTION

Burnout is a pervasive and chronic stress response, usually to workplace conditions. It can feel physically, mentally, emotionally, and spiritually exhausting. It can leave you unable to access inner resources, and it can erode your self-confidence and trust in the world around you. It can happen to anyone. Perhaps it is happening to you.

If so, you have lots of company. A 2018 burnout survey conducted by "Big Four" accounting firm Deloitte found that "77 percent of respondents say they have experienced employee burnout at their current job, with more than half citing more than one occurrence."[1]

But here's the good news: Recovery from burnout is within your reach. You've got the field guide in your hands. Journal therapy is an effective and accessible way to write yourself into a greater sense of well-being, and new research in brain science tells us that well-being is a skill that can be learned.

In this book, work is defined as "any regular skilled activities that produce goods or services, whether paid or unpaid." Burnout can and does happen not only to office workers. Parents, homeschoolers, caregivers, and volunteers can all experience burnout. You can be susceptible to burnout whether you are unemployed, a gig economy worker, an entrepreneur, an on-call worker, or a full-time artist, writer, musician, or actor. Burnout can happen even when you love the work you do. And as we know from the COVID-19 pandemic, just the struggle to get through day-to-day life can make us susceptible to burnout.

I define *journal therapy* as the purposeful and intentional use of writing to support self-directed change. Writing in a purposeful and intentional way has many benefits. The social science research of Dr. James Pennebaker[2] and his associates demonstrates over and over the physiologically and emotionally healing properties of writing. These properties include the capacity to develop a cohesive, coherent story about a stressful or traumatic event, which aids in making meaning; improved immune system functioning; and fewer visits to health care professionals for stress-related illnesses.

---

1. Jen Fisher, "Workplace Burnout Survey," Deloitte, accessed June 14, 2021, https://www2.deloitte.com/us/en/pages/about-deloitte/articles/burnout-survey.html.
2. James W. Pennebaker, *Writing to Heal: A Guided Journal for Recovering from Trauma & Emotional Upheaval.* (Lakewood, CO: Center for Journal Therapy, 2013).

Pennebaker writes: "Emotional writing can also [positively] affect people's sleep habits, work efficiency, and how they connect to others. Indeed, when we put our traumatic experiences into words, we tend to become less concerned with the emotional events that have been weighing us down." [3]

This book provides six different approaches for restoring balance and peace of mind through journal writing and prompts from experts on burnout recovery and journal therapy. You'll find writing processes that harness the brain's neuroplasticity, or its capacity to change itself based on experience; explore workplace transitions; build habits that support wellness; and learn ways to simplify different aspects of your life. You'll use animal metaphors and practice writing techniques that help you make behavioral and emotional shifts.

When completed sequentially over 12 or more months, these prompts can help you recover from burnout, shift your relationship toward your work through a step-by-step process, and actively engage with your own well-being.

Again, well-being is a skill that can be learned. That's what the research of neuroplasticity experts Drs. Cortland Dahl, Christine Wilson-Mendenhall, and Richard Davidson found. In a 2020 study,[4] they lay out four pillars of well-being—awareness, connection, insight, and purpose—that can be cultivated through "intentional mental training" and by learning "innovative solutions to strengthen" the skills of well-being.

This book offers this mental training and these innovative solutions. The strategies you will use to overcome burnout and cultivate well-being come from these fields:

- **NEUROPLASTICITY** ❖ Neuroplasticity is the way your brain creates new neural pathways to shape itself based on your lived experience, for better or worse. Whether the shaping is for enhancing well-being or for reinforcing self-defeating thoughts depends on where you place your attention over time. Deborah Ross, a licensed professional counselor and certified journal therapist, offers an instruction manual to your brain.

3. James W. Pennebaker, *Writing to Heal: A Guided Journal for Recovering from Trauma & Emotional Upheaval.* (Lakewood, CO: Center for Journal Therapy, 2013).
4. Cortland J. Dahl, Christine Wilson-Mendenhall, and Richard J. Davidson, "The Plasticity of Well-being: A Training-based Framework for the Cultivation of Human Flourishing." *Proceedings of the National Academy of Sciences of the United States of America* 117, no. 51 (December 2020): 32197–32206.

She shows how you can use writing to deepen the installation of the thoughts, habits, behaviors, and emotions for better well-being.

- **TRANSITIONS** ❖ Transitions are life stages that bridge us from "letting go of the old way" through the "messy middle of the in-between" to the "new way." Change is inevitable in life, and transitions are the way that we respond to changes. These prompts are from Leia Francisco, a board-certified business coach and a certified poetry and journal facilitator, who will help you let go, manage the middle, and step confidently into the new way.

- **WELLNESS** ❖ Abundant seeds of pragmatic, science-backed best practices for wellness and well-being during burnout recovery are planted throughout this book. These wellness skills cover everything from the basics—including tips on sleep, nutrition, hydration, and breath—to emotional, mental, and mindfulness strategies. These prompts come from Nancy Scherlong, a licensed clinical social worker, certified journal therapist, and registered poetry therapist whose expertise is in helping individuals, groups, and organizations to change their stories through holistic physical, emotional, and mental health shifts.

- **SIMPLICITY** ❖ One common symptom of burnout is a pervasive sense of overwhelm. Cultivating simplicity by clearing physical, emotional, mental, and time clutter reduces overwhelm and restores clarity and spaciousness to your environment, heart, mind, and spirit. Carolyn Koehnline, a licensed mental health counselor and certified journal therapist, will expertly guide you through the complexities of achieving simplicity.

- **ANIMAL WISDOM** ❖ Your brain loves both metaphor and novelty, and the wisdom of the finned, furred, feathered, and footed brings notes of surprise and integration, two enhancements to well-being, to this journal. Linda Barnes, certified journal and poetry facilitator, is a lifelong friend of the animal kingdom. As a published poet and poetry teacher, she is fluent in the languages of both animals and metaphor.

- **JOURNAL** ❖ The journal can be a friend in need, a sounding board, a loyal companion, an incubator for new behaviors, and a record of your journey to well-being. The prompts in this category offer tools, tips, and techniques for maximum effectiveness of all the prompts. They come from me, Kathleen Adams, a licensed professional counselor and registered poetry and journal therapist. Since 1985, my life's work has been discovering how and why journal writing brings recovery and well-being to those who suffer or struggle.

It is the collective hope of the contributors that, week by week, you will find your way through burnout to well-being, a skill that can be—and, a year from now, you will have—learned.

—Kathleen Adams, LPC
Registered Poetry/Journal Therapist

HOW TO GAIN THE MOST FROM THIS JOURNAL

This journal offers a yearlong study of strategies and best practices for overcoming burnout. For best results, keep the following guidelines in mind:

✳ Work at your own pace. You do not need to write every day, but you'll have the best outcomes if you follow the prompts sequentially, even if you have days between entries.

✳ Plan to spend about 5 to 10 minutes per prompt. If you want to write more or less, feel free. If a length shorter or longer than 5 to 10 minutes is recommended, it will be stated in the prompt. Save 2 or 3 minutes at the end of each entry to read through your writing and harvest your insights in a reflection write (see Week 2, Day 2 to learn more).

✳ In this book, the word *write* is both a verb and a noun. As a noun ("Read back your *write* and reflect on it"), it represents the journal prompt you have just completed.

✳ You are welcome to skip any prompt that you feel isn't relevant or is overly provocative. Dr. Pennebaker's "Flip-Out Rule" offers a guideline: If you start to flip out, or think you might, stop writing.[5]

✳ The book is constructed so you can use its pages for your writing. However, you may prefer to keep a separate journal, either in a physical notebook or in a digital file. It will be helpful to date your pages and include the week and day numbers for easy cross-referencing.

---

5. James W. Pennebaker, *Writing to Heal: A Guided Journal for Recovering from Trauma & Emotional Upheaval* (Lakewood, CO: Center for Journal Therapy, 2013), 23.

✳ There is no significant difference in outcomes between writing by hand and writing by keyboard. Do what feels easiest or most natural to you.

✳ In the course of this exploration, you may come to realize that your burnout recovery would benefit from outside support. Please seek professional help if needed.

Whether you're a novice writer or an experienced journaler, you may not have gone through a structured writing program that expertly guides you across an entire year. Thus, the first week orients you to the basic journal-writing practices and techniques that we'll use throughout the book.

Starting with Week 2, the first day of each week has been reserved for setting intentions. Day 3 of each week is reserved for a one-year journey through transitions, and Day 4 is similarly reserved for lessons and prompts on neuroplasticity. Day 7 offers a review of the week, with questions for self-evaluation so that you can track your progress over time. Days 2, 5, and 6 feature rotating themes on journaling (which are always on Day 2 when they appear), animal wisdom, simplicity, and wellness. All themes compound over time, offering you opportunities to chart and track your progress.

The famous diarist Anaïs Nin wrote: "Life shrinks or expands in proportion to one's courage."[6] Thank you for your courage in undertaking a program that we sincerely hope will offer life-expanding opportunities for growth, positive change, restored balance and increased inner peace. Write on!

---

6. Anaïs Nin, *The Diaries of Anaïs Nin, Vol 3: 1939–1944* (New York: Houghton Mifflin, 2009), 125.

WELCOME ❖ "YOU" IN THREE MINUTES. Let's start with you. What's your story? Set your watch or phone timer for three minutes and answer the questions below.

WRITE ON! Who are you? Why have you chosen this burnout recovery program? What do you want to be different and better, a year from now? Bulleted lists are fine, as are fragments or random bursts of words. Just get your thoughts down.

_____

_____

_____

_____

_____

_____

_____

JOURNAL ❖ REFLECTION. The reflection write is a key tool in the journal toolbox. After you've responded to a daily prompt, the process of reading it back to yourself and then writing a sentence or two of feedback harvests insight and brings clarity.

WRITE ON! Read back the story you wrote yesterday. Then write a sentence or two of feedback, starting with "As I read this, I notice . . .," or "I'm surprised by . . .," or "I'm curious about . . . ."

_____

_____

_____

_____

_____

_____

JOURNAL ❖ FOR YOUR EYES ONLY. Your journal is your private book or digital file. No one has the right to read it without your permission. If your family respects boundaries, tell them you are writing a burnout journal and ask them to not snoop. Otherwise, try a digital journal in the cloud, a password-protected app, obscurely named folders, or a flash drive. In a paper journal, you might write "Private!" on the cover and first page. Stash it in your book bag, backpack, or a locking file drawer.

WRITE ON! How will you protect your privacy? Write for five minutes. Reflect.

_____

_____

_____

_____

_____

_____

_____

_____

_____

_____

_____

_____

_____

_____

_____

_____

_____

_____

_____

_____

JOURNAL ❖ THE "RULES." Your journal doesn't care if your writing is sloppy. If you can't spell, that's okay. You don't have to be a "good writer" or write every day. You can write by hand or on a keyboard. If there is one guideline to follow, it's this: date your entries, including the year. Otherwise, there are no rules!

WRITE ON! Are there "rules" about journal writing that inhibit you? Write them down. Can you release them? Scribble over them!

_____

_____

_____

_____

_____

_____

_____

_____

_____

_____

_____

_____

_____

_____

_____

_____

_____

_____

_____

JOURNAL ❖ YOUR JOURNAL AS RECOVERY INCUBATOR. Your journal is a friend in need, a time machine, a grounding rod, a bridge, and an incubator for the hard yet transformative work of burnout recovery.

WRITE ON! Today, continue what you started on Day 1. Write more specifically about your hopes and desires for the year ahead. Who do you want to be, what do you want to be doing, and what do you hope to have by the time you reach the 366th writing prompt? What will be different and better at the end of this incubation?

_____

_____

_____

_____

_____

_____

_____

_____

_____

_____

_____

_____

_____

_____

_____

_____

_____

_____

_____

_____

JOURNAL ❖ FIVE-MINUTE SPRINT. It's just like it sounds: five minutes of quick writing, set on a timer. Five minutes is the standard suggested writing time for this journal, because it is a manageable time frame that yields a surprising amount of information and insight. Write more or less if you wish. Add two minutes after your sprint to read back and reflect on your writing.

WRITE ON! Close your eyes. Check in with your body. What do you feel? Where do you feel it? Set your timer for five minutes and write. Read and reflect. What do you notice?

_____

_____

_____

_____

_____

_____

JOURNAL ❖ SENTENCE STEMS. Sometimes even a five-minute sprint is too much. That's when we bust out sentence stems. Start a sentence and let yourself complete it once or many times. Work quickly to encourage spontaneity.

WRITE ON! Make a list of sentence stems, starting with "I want . . .," "The most important thing is . . .," and "Burnout is. . . ." Add three more of your own. Finish your own sentence stems, completing each one once or offering several answers for each. Reflect on your responses.

_____

_____

_____

_____

_____

_____

INTENTIONS ❖ Intentions are outcomes we envision and move toward. While goals are often externally driven, intentions tend to be internally sourced. Since a large part of burnout is feeling out of control, intentions help you stay focused on what really matters to you. Moving forward, you'll write three intentions on the first day of each week.

WRITE ON! What are three intentions for this week? They could be practical: "Reclaim control by clearing the paper from my desk." They could be restorative: "Read for pleasure every day." What will help you structure time, energy, and focus for the best outcomes?

_____

_____

_____

_____

_____

_____

WELLNESS ❖ WHAT IS WELLNESS? Wellness is a state of balance in mind, body, heart, and spirit resulting in a state of internal peace and harmony, or flow. Even when life is stressful, there is relief available through practices such as basic self-care (healthy sleep, hydration, nutrition, breathwork); connected relationships; access to pleasure and fun; purposeful work or activity; and paying attention to inner guidance. We'll explore all these dimensions of wellness.

WRITE ON! Take inventory. In what areas of your life do you experience wellness? In what areas is it lacking? Write for five minutes. Read and reflect.

_____

_____

_____

_____

_____

TRANSITION ❖ YOU'RE IN TRANSITION. Change happens to all of us. Sometimes it's planned. Often it's sudden and unexpected. A transition is how you manage a change. All transitions have three phases: (1) You let go of what used to be; (2) You move through an in-between of not-knowing; (3) You live into and accept the new way. You may not have control of change, but you can take control of your transition.

WRITE ON! What is one transition you have successfully completed? Think back and identify the three stages. Describe how you managed each stage.

_____

_____

_____

_____

_____

_____

_____

_____

_____

_____

_____

_____

_____

_____

_____

_____

_____

_____

_____

_____

NEUROPLASTICITY ❖ YOUR BRAIN AS ALLY. One of your allies on this journey to burnout recovery is your miraculous brain. As discussed in the Introduction, the research of Drs. Dahl, Wilson-Mendenhall, and Davidson reveals that well-being is a skill that can be learned. This learning process can change your brain through better-feeling thoughts, more harmony and ease, and a clearer sense of agency over your own life.

WRITE ON! What is your reaction to this news that well-being is a skill that can be learned? Write for five minutes and reflect.

_____

_____

_____

_____

_____

_____

_____

_____

_____

_____

_____

_____

_____

_____

_____

_____

SIMPLICITY ❖ A GENTLE APPROACH TO CLUTTER. Clutter is the excess baggage that accumulates in your home, head, heart, and schedule. It can drain energy, scatter focus, weigh you down, block progress, and distract you from your priorities. For many people, the circumstances leading to burnout are a breeding ground for not just physical clutter, but also mental, emotional, and even time clutter. We'll explore each type throughout the journal.

WRITE ON! Today, write for five minutes about your current clutter situation. Is there one kind of clutter—physical, mental, emotional, time—that stands out for you? Read and reflect.

_____

_____

_____

_____

_____

_____

_____

_____

_____

_____

_____

_____

_____

_____

_____

_____

_____

_____

ANIMAL WISDOM ❖ YOUR ANIMAL TEACHERS. An animal teacher is any animal that infuses the universe with its wisdom. None is superior, as each has its place. We will use animal metaphors throughout this journal to discover clever and creative ways that the habits of finned, feathered, furred, and footed friends can speak to your recovery.

WRITE ON! Think about a creature from the animal kingdom that might represent your burnout. Are you the Hamster furiously spinning in your wheel? Or are you a Turtle: frantically pulling inward to your shell? Write for five minutes, read back, and reflect.

_____

_____

_____

_____

_____

WEEKLY REVIEW ❖ Read back the week's entries, reflections, or both. How do you rank your burnout this week? How do you rank your satisfaction with the writing process? Are you noticing small shifts?

WRITE ON! On a scale of 1 (low) to 7 (high), rate your week:

Burnout?	①	②	③	④	⑤	⑥	⑦
Writing process?	①	②	③	④	⑤	⑥	⑦
Noticing changes?	①	②	③	④	⑤	⑥	⑦

WRITE ON! Write observations as you rate your week. Note connections and changes from last week. Reflect on anything else you notice or that surprises you.

_____

_____

_____

_____

_____

INTENTIONS ❖ Setting weekly intentions helps you focus and organize your week around outcomes that really matter to you. Your intentions may include goals or objectives that will help you meet deadlines and stay true to your commitments.

WRITE ON! What are three intentions for this week? What is the feeling you will experience when you manifest these intentions?

_____

_____

_____

_____

_____

_____

_____

JOURNAL ❖ LISTS. Lists are a wonderfully versatile journaling technique. They're great for corralling information and can help you stay focused. In this journal, we will be using short lists, usually with ten or fewer entries. (Do be careful to keep your to-do lists reasonable.)

WRITE ON! Let's practice writing short lists! Make three lists: ten things you are glad to have in your life, five things you'd like to get rid of, and three awesome things about yourself. To practice deepening your writing, choose anything from your lists and write about it for five minutes. Read back and reflect.

_____

_____

_____

_____

_____

_____

TRANSITIONS ❖ WHAT IS WORK BURNOUT? Herein, work is defined as any regularly performed skilled activities that offer services or goods, whether paid or unpaid. Unpaid work can include caretaking, working in the home, volunteering, or serving on committees, task forces, or boards. Work can also include any other circumstance, such as being unemployed and job-seeking, that causes prolonged stress on your time, energy, and focus. Any work, however defined, can cause burnout in your body and mind.

WRITE ON! What is your work? What are its sources of stress? What are your physical, mental, and emotional responses to this stress?

_____

_____

_____

_____

_____

_____

_____

_____

_____

_____

_____

_____

_____

_____

_____

_____

_____

_____

NEUROPLASTICITY ❖ YOUR BRAIN AND YOUR MIND. According to Dr. Rick Hanson, your brain takes the shape that your mind rests upon. When you focus on the negative, you feed burnout. When you focus on more purposeful thoughts, you feed positive brain change. Guide your brain toward well-being.

WRITE ON! Look back at your intentions for this week. Write and reflect on the idea that you can feed these intentions with conscious thought and purposeful activity.

ANIMAL WISDOM ❖ DO IT NOW. Have you ever watched Antelope racing and leaping? There is a breathtaking beauty in taking sudden action. Like Antelope, sometimes you can outpace and leave burnout behind by taking bold forward strides.

WRITE ON! Yesterday, you wrote about feeding your intentions with conscious thought and purposeful activity. Today, write about taking a conscious step or leap. What can you do, whether bold or simple, to move in the direction of your purposeful intention?

_____

_____

_____

_____

_____

_____

_____

_____

_____

_____

_____

_____

_____

_____

_____

_____

_____

_____

_____

_____

WELLNESS ❖ MIND (TOO) FULL. Part of the cognitive overwhelm of burnout relates to having too much on your mind. Mindfulness helps soothe and empty a too-full mind by encouraging you to experience the present moment through all five senses, without judgment. Sound hard? Starting small helps! Practice this sensory grounding technique in brief bursts.

WRITE ON! Breathe deeply and write down five things you see, four things you hear, three things you touch, two things you smell, and one thing you taste. When you are finished, read back and reflect.

_____

_____

_____

_____

_____

WEEKLY REVIEW ❖ Read back the week's entries, reflections, or both. How do you rank your burnout this week? How do you rank your satisfaction with the writing process? How is the realistic progress of your intentions? Are you noticing shifts from prior weeks?

On a scale of 1 (low) to 7 (high), rate your week:

Burnout?	①	②	③	④	⑤	⑥	⑦
Writing process?	①	②	③	④	⑤	⑥	⑦
Intentions?	①	②	③	④	⑤	⑥	⑦
Noticing changes?	①	②	③	④	⑤	⑥	⑦

WRITE ON! Write observations as you rate your week. Note any connections you may see.

_____

_____

_____

_____

DATE _____

INTENTIONS ❖ Intentions bring focus and awareness to your days. Your intentions guide your actions. Your actions bring you closer to what you want.

WRITE ON! Write three intentions for this week, taking note of one or two actions you could take for each.

_____

_____

_____

_____

_____

_____

_____

DATE _____

ANIMAL WISDOM ❖ YOUR "I DID" LIST. Blue Jay notices every detail. Changes in the environment invite curiosity and closer inspection. Many a tidbit is a treasure. Like Blue Jay, you can find tiny successes to reinforce self-reliance, a key to burnout recovery.

WRITE ON! At the end of the day, get curious and write an "I Did" list of the tasks that you started and completed. Brushing your teeth, making phone calls, fixing a snack, opening the mail, writing a section of a report—take note of all the tidbits, no matter how small, and reflect.

_____

_____

_____

_____

_____

_____

TRANSITIONS ❖ THE PRICE OF BURNOUT. A 2018 Gallup survey of full-time workers found that two-thirds experienced burnout. Common symptoms include feeling used up, bored, depleted, disengaged, chronically fatigued, conflicted, or consistently unhappy with the workplace. Dissatisfaction with a workplace's environment, culture, required tasks, or dynamic carries a price: feeling insufficient, joyless, or stressed.

WRITE ON! List your burnout symptoms, including any not listed above. Rank them in order of how much they cost you. Choose one of the higher ranked symptoms. Write about the price you pay. Read back and reflect.

NEUROPLASTICITY ❖ AWARENESS. The first pillar of well-being from the research of Dahl, Wilson-Mendenhall, and Davidson is awareness. Before you can make intentional change, you must first be able to notice and observe thoughts, feelings, and behaviors. When you practice awareness, you learn to focus your attention.

WRITE ON! Where is your mind right now? Place attention and focus on your thoughts and state of mind. Set your timer for five minutes and write what you notice. Start with "My mind is. . . ." Midway, shift to this question: "Where would I like my mind to be?" Read back and reflect.

_____

_____

_____

_____

_____

_____

_____

_____

_____

_____

_____

_____

_____

_____

_____

_____

_____

_____

SIMPLICITY ❖ A SIMPLER SPACE. To reduce the overwhelm that comes with burnout, it helps to have living and working spaces that work with you, not against you. Physical clutter, such as the papers and objects that cover your surfaces and crowd your corners, can keep you from feeling at home.

WRITE ON! Imagine a living or working space that would help you feel and function your best. What is one kind of physical clutter you would need to clear? If your living space is not your own or can't be easily changed, can you visualize an uncluttered space where you can internally retreat?

_____

_____

_____

_____

_____

_____

_____

_____

_____

_____

_____

_____

_____

_____

_____

_____

_____

_____

_____

WELLNESS ❖ EAT THAT ELEPHANT. Desmond Tutu once said, "There is only one way to eat an Elephant: a bite at a time." Breaking down complex tasks into smaller steps helps you start a project and increase your hope about completing it.

WRITE ON! Think of a project or task—small, like laundry, or big, like filing taxes. Break it into small actionable steps. Can you take the first step today? How will it feel when you've taken that first bite?

_____

_____

_____

_____

WEEKLY REVIEW ❖ Read back the week's entries, reflections, or both. How do you rank your burnout this week? How do you rank your satisfaction with the writing process? How is the realistic progress of your intentions? Are you noticing changes?

On a scale of 1 (low) to 7 (high), rate your week:

Burnout?	①	②	③	④	⑤	⑥	⑦
Writing process?	①	②	③	④	⑤	⑥	⑦
Intentions?	①	②	③	④	⑤	⑥	⑦
Noticing changes?	①	②	③	④	⑤	⑥	⑦

WRITE ON! Write observations as you rate your week. Note any connections you may see. Look back over the last four weeks and compare your ratings. Are you noticing progress?

_____

_____

_____

_____

DATE _____

INTENTIONS ❖ It's time to write intentions! What are three things you'd like to complete or resolve this week?

WRITE ON! What are three intentions for this week? Remember to keep them week-sized.

_____

_____

_____

_____

_____

_____

_____

_____

DATE _____

ANIMAL WISDOM ❖ **ROLL UP YOUR SLEEVES.** Beavers are the engineers of the animal world. They can turn a grove of trees beside a trickling stream into a stout home with a family swimming pool. Careful engineering can be an asset in burnout recovery. Assess your raw materials, like time, talent, and knowledge. Use this inventory to engineer a project in advance.

WRITE ON! Think of a postponed task that needs 15–30 focused minutes—an email, some budgeting or bookkeeping, or a phone call. Write down the task and desired outcome. Put it on your calendar. Upon completion, reflect.

_____

_____

_____

_____

_____

TRANSITIONS ❖ NAME YOUR TRANSITION. Think of a positive transition that could help banish work burnout. (Remember, work can be whatever purposeful activity you pursue, in or out of the home, with or without pay.) What would be different and better? The hours? Workload? Type of work? Your circumstances? Give a name to the desired transition, such as "More Time for Me," "Better Teamwork," or "Back on My Feet."

WRITE ON! Write the name of your desired transition, then write about the meaning behind the choice.

_____
_____
_____
_____
_____
_____
_____
_____
_____
_____
_____
_____
_____
_____
_____
_____
_____
_____
_____
_____

NEUROPLASTICITY ❖ CONNECTION. Connection, the second pillar of well-being, helps your brain remember that there is strength in numbers, particularly with loved ones. "Loved ones" may include anyone or anything that enlivens you, such as people, animals, wildlife, nature, ideas, passion projects, causes, and real or vividly imagined places.

WRITE ON! In the middle of a page, write down and circle "My Loved Ones." Write names and associations around the circle. Notice your feelings as you draw a line between each and the center circle. Step back and take in your web of connections visually. Reflect on what you notice.

_____
_____
_____
_____
_____
_____
_____
_____
_____
_____
_____
_____
_____
_____
_____
_____
_____
_____
_____
_____

SIMPLICITY ❖ A SIMPLIFIED SCHEDULE. An overscheduled calendar contributes to burnout by setting an expectation that you can do more than is reasonable. It takes clarity and courage to cut out time wasters. When you do, you will find more room for rhythms of restoration, meaningful connections, and purposeful endeavors. Start by sorting out what matters to you.

WRITE ON! Write this sentence ten times. Then fill in the blanks: "I want to spend less time _____ and more time _____." Review and reflect on your answers.

_____

_____

_____

_____

_____

_____

_____

_____

_____

_____

_____

_____

_____

_____

_____

_____

_____

_____

_____

_____

WELLNESS ❖ HYDRATE YOUR STRESS. We often don't recognize the cues of thirst or set up our environment with readily available healthy liquids. But health journalist Gina Shaw reports that drinking water during difficult times can lower cortisol, the primary stress hormone.

WRITE ON! What are the most stressful times of day for you? Where are you? How could you make water or herbal teas more available in these places? Write a short action plan.

_____

_____

_____

_____

_____

_____

WEEKLY REVIEW ❖ Read back the week's entries, reflections, or both. How do you rank your burnout this week? How do you rank your satisfaction with the writing process? How is the realistic progress of your intentions? Are you noticing changes?

On a scale of 1 (low) to 7 (high), rate your week:

Burnout?	①	②	③	④	⑤	⑥	⑦
Writing process?	①	②	③	④	⑤	⑥	⑦
Intentions?	①	②	③	④	⑤	⑥	⑦
Noticing changes?	①	②	③	④	⑤	⑥	⑦

WRITE ON! Write observations as you rate your week. Note any connections you may see.

_____

_____

_____

_____

INTENTIONS ❖ Perhaps you are getting into the rhythm of writing three intentions for the week. Are your intentions focused enough to make significant progress in seven days?

WRITE ON! What are three intentions for this week? See if you can keep them manageable for a week.

_____

_____

_____

_____

_____

_____

_____

JOURNAL ❖ THREE FEELING WORDS. Feelings are fickle; they change with time and process. Writing is a process that can shift feelings quickly. Before you write, describe your current feeling state in three words or phrases at the top of the page. After you complete the reflection, write down three feeling words or phrases and compare the results.

WRITE ON! Try it! First, consider the prompt, "What's on my mind?" Then write three feeling words and write to the prompt for five minutes. Read and reflect, then note three more feeling words. Compare them. Are there shifts or surprises?

_____

_____

_____

_____

_____

_____

TRANSITIONS ❖ GETTING SPECIFIC. Imagine your typical week. Think about the tasks you perform, the people you interact with, and how you deal with unexpected situations. Can you think of recent examples of feeling bored, used up, or overwhelmed?

WRITE ON! As specifically as you can, list those tasks, people, environments, or circumstances that drain and stress you. Read over the list and put checks by the ones that most deplete you. Are there patterns? Surprises? Confirmations? Reflect on what you notice.

_____

_____

_____

_____

_____

_____

_____

_____

_____

_____

_____

_____

_____

_____

_____

_____

_____

_____

_____

_____

_____

NEUROPLASTICITY ❖ INSIGHT. Dahl, Wilson-Mendenhall, and Davidson describe insight, the third pillar of well-being, as awareness of how your thoughts, feelings, beliefs, and experiences shape you. This self-awareness informs your sense of self and how you relate to the world. Let's say you feel anxious about giving a speech. Insight helps you notice any thoughts that you might "mess up" or "make a fool of yourself," then recognize those thoughts as self-defeating.

WRITE ON! The reflection write offers an excellent way to practice cultivating insight. Today, write about what you are learning from your reflections. Reflect on your reflections only if you wish!

_____

_____

_____

_____

_____

_____

_____

_____

_____

_____

_____

_____

_____

_____

_____

_____

_____

_____

SIMPLICITY ❖ MENTAL CLARITY. A clear mind makes it easier to navigate the mix of stressors life can deliver. When things get overwhelming, mental clutter can replace useful thinking with endless worry, negative self-talk, overanalyzing, or attempts to control uncontrollable things or solve all problems at once.

WRITE ON! What type of mental clutter are you most prone to experience? Write about your personal mental clutter, including some of the self-talk that drives it. Read back and reflect.

_____

_____

_____

_____

_____

_____

_____

_____

_____

_____

_____

_____

_____

_____

_____

_____

_____

_____

_____

_____

_____

DATE _____

ANIMAL WISDOM ❖ SEEK COOPERATION. The power of Ant comes from cooperation. Together, Ants can move a mountain or devour an entire forest. Working as part of a cooperating team reduces burnout and makes tasks and projects fun instead of frazzling.

WRITE ON! Make a list of everyone who could serve as an ally for a task or project. Plan how you will reach out and ask for cooperation from them. Perhaps offer something in return!

_____

_____

_____

_____

_____

_____

DATE _____

WEEKLY REVIEW ❖ Read back the week's entries, reflections, or both. How do you rank your burnout this week? How do you rank your satisfaction with the writing process? How is the realistic progress of your intentions? Are you noticing changes?

On a scale of 1 (low) to 7 (high), rate your week:

Burnout?	①	②	③	④	⑤	⑥	⑦
Writing process?	①	②	③	④	⑤	⑥	⑦
Intentions?	①	②	③	④	⑤	⑥	⑦
Noticing changes?	①	②	③	④	⑤	⑥	⑦

WRITE ON! Write observations as you rate your week. Note any connections you may see.

_____

_____

_____

_____

INTENTIONS ❖ How are your intentions coming along? Is it getting easier to discern which are internally sourced intentions and which are deadline-driven or otherwise externally sourced goals? Both are fine to set as weekly intentions.

WRITE ON! List your three intentions for this week. These can be related to any area of your life. Break larger intentions into week-sized bites.

_____

_____

_____

_____

_____

_____

_____

JOURNAL ❖ **WHY WRITING WORKS.** You've been writing for six weeks. Perhaps you've observed that writing is helping you clarify, codify, and synthesize different aspects of your stress and burnout. Over the next few months, we'll explore why writing works as a cognitive, emotional, behavioral, and mindfulness tool.

WRITE ON! What are you noticing so far about the effectiveness of your writing?

_____

_____

_____

_____

_____

_____

_____

TRANSITIONS ❖ READY TO LET GO? Letting go is the first stage of a transition. To start your work transition from burnout to recovery, you must release things that exhaust and stress you. Some endings are easier and happen quickly. Others require more time. You do not have to let go of everything at once.

WRITE ON! What aspects of your work transition can you release? They can be concrete, like an uncomfortable desk chair, or intangible, like a toxic workplace relationship. Choose the most challenging item. Write about its impact on you. What would help you let it go?

_____

_____

_____

_____

_____

_____

_____

_____

_____

_____

_____

_____

_____

_____

_____

_____

_____

_____

_____

_____

_____

_____

DATE _____

NEUROPLASTICITY ❖ PURPOSE. Dahl, Wilson-Mendenhall, and Davidson define purpose, the fourth pillar of well-being, as clarity about "personally meaningful aims and values" that you can apply and embody. With purpose, your life has meaning and significance. When you face challenges, you persevere. You develop behaviors and habits that help you serve your higher purpose.

WRITE ON! What purposes give your life meaning? Do any of these purposes contribute to your sense of burnout? If so, how? Which ones are life-sustaining? What can you do to reclaim your purpose-filled activities as meaning-making rather than stress-inducing?

_____

_____

_____

_____

_____

_____

_____

_____

_____

_____

_____

_____

_____

_____

_____

_____

_____

_____

_____

SIMPLICITY ❖ BITE-SIZED TRANSFORMATIONS. When you're feeling burned out and overwhelmed, life feels chaotic. Today, you'll focus on bite-sized chaotic spaces to transform.

WRITE ON! Write a list of ten tiny spaces that frustrate you on a regular basis—a bedside table, a glove compartment, your computer desktop. Circle one. Give it 10 minutes today. Then write a brief report and reflection.

_____

_____

_____

_____

_____

_____

_____

_____

_____

_____

_____

_____

_____

_____

_____

_____

_____

_____

_____

_____

_____

_____

_____

WELLNESS ❖ MEDIA FAST. Compassion fatigue expert Charles Figley suggests taking breaks from media or news when you feel overwhelmed by negative inputs. Learning to change the channel or stop the scroll, he says, can help you focus more on what is most important to you.

WRITE ON! First, list the various media outlets where you get your news. How can you reduce your exposure to difficult news? Write down your strategies. Then note two or three ways you could repurpose your newfound time.

_____

_____

_____

_____

_____

_____

WEEKLY REVIEW ❖ Read back the week's entries, reflections, or both. How do you rank your burnout this week? How do you rank your satisfaction with the writing process? How is the realistic progress of your intentions? Are you noticing changes?

On a scale of 1 (low) to 7 (high), rate your week:

Burnout?	① ② ③ ④ ⑤ ⑥ ⑦
Writing process?	① ② ③ ④ ⑤ ⑥ ⑦
Intentions?	① ② ③ ④ ⑤ ⑥ ⑦
Noticing changes?	① ② ③ ④ ⑤ ⑥ ⑦

WRITE ON! Write observations as you rate your week. Note any connections you may see.

_____

_____

_____

_____

INTENTIONS ❖ You've been writing intentions for two months now. Are you noticing progress? Look back at some of your early weeks and notice if there are any unresolved intentions. Do they still matter?

WRITE ON! If appropriate, carry forward some unresolved intentions and see if you can move them to the "actualized" column. If you're caught up, write three week-sized intentions and reflect on the intention-setting process so far.

_____

_____

_____

_____

_____

_____

JOURNAL ❖ **CLUSTERING.** Clustering is also known as mind-mapping. It can generate insight quickly. It starts with a circled word or phrase in the middle of a page. Lines radiate out in any order, each with a circled association to a thought, feeling, or experience. A line connects each tier of associations to its spinoff. For fresh associations, return to center.

WRITE ON! Try clustering by using "My burnout" as the central phrase. Work quickly. Don't edit or censor; just get your associations down. When you're done, sit back and observe. Write a synthesis of what you notice and any insights.

_____

_____

_____

_____

_____

_____

TRANSITIONS ❖ SURROUND YOURSELF WITH SUPPORT. In the letting-go stage, create a transition team of helpers. It can include a coworker, mentor, friend, family, team member, helping professional, clergy, support group leader, or anyone else that you trust to support your recovery and well-being. "Team members" can also include music, exercise, meditation, pets, and nature. Each brings something special to your transition.

WRITE ON! Write a list of all the supports you can surround yourself with. Hard to ask for help? You're not alone. Add one at a time if you feel hesitant. Tell each exactly how they can help you. Then let them help!

_____

_____

_____

_____

_____

_____

_____

_____

_____

_____

_____

_____

_____

_____

_____

_____

_____

_____

_____

_____

NEUROPLASTICITY ❖ NAME IT TO TAME IT. Psychiatrist Daniel J. Siegel coined the phrase "name it to tame it" to describe an important neuroplasticity principle. Naming is powerful for gaining a sense of mastery or control over burnout.

WRITE ON! Try on some names for your burnout recovery process. Name them in the style of *Friends* episodes, like "The One about _____." Or try a poetic bent, like "Life Between the Trapezes." Or be straightforward, as in "A Year to Better Health." Choose one and use it as a title. Then write the story that goes with the name. Reflect.

_____

_____

_____

_____

_____

_____

_____

_____

_____

_____

_____

_____

_____

_____

_____

_____

_____

_____

_____

_____

SIMPLICITY ❖ A "DO-ABLE" DAY. Do you wake up instantly exhausted and overwhelmed by a tightly packed agenda? That's called time clutter, and it's a demoralizing start to the day. There's much you probably can't control about your calendar, but you can have some effect on how "do-able" your day is.

WRITE ON! Start with, *Today I'm going to make my day more do-able.* Then write for five minutes describing how you will achieve that. Can you remove one item? Put space between commitments? Get help with a complex project? Reflect. Then take the first step.

_____

_____

_____

_____

_____

_____

_____

_____

_____

_____

_____

_____

_____

_____

_____

_____

_____

_____

_____

_____

_____

WELLNESS ❖ WHAT'S YOUR STORY? Our "narrative," or how we speak to ourselves, can often fuel our feelings. Are you a caring person who tells yourself, "If I don't help out this person, then I'm not doing enough?" Do you tell yourself scary stories about not performing perfectly? If your narrative brings stress with it, take a closer look at it.

WRITE ON! Write down what you tell yourself about your commitments and obligations. Which of these messages are true? Which may be based in an old story? Choose two items and turn them into more balanced, realistic statements.

_____

_____

_____

_____

WEEKLY REVIEW ❖ Read back the week's entries, reflections, or both. How do you rank your burnout this week? How do you rank your satisfaction with the writing process? How is the progress of your intentions? Are you noticing changes?

On a scale of 1 (low) to 7 (high), rate your week:

Burnout?	①	②	③	④	⑤	⑥	⑦
Writing process?	①	②	③	④	⑤	⑥	⑦
Intentions?	①	②	③	④	⑤	⑥	⑦
Noticing changes?	①	②	③	④	⑤	⑥	⑦

WRITE ON! Write observations as you rate your week. Note any connections you may see. Look back over the last four weeks and compare your ratings. Are you noticing progress?

_____

_____

_____

_____

DATE _____

INTENTIONS ❖ Eight weeks in, your weekly intention-setting is becoming a habit. Every time you continue writing weekly intentions, the practice will deepen and become more natural.

WRITE ON! What are three intentions for this week? Keep them specific enough so you can make observable progress in a week.

_____

_____

_____

_____

_____

_____

DATE _____

ANIMAL WISDOM ❖ A PLAYFUL SPIRIT. Otters are renowned for their sense of play. They slide down riverbanks to splash into the water repeatedly. They revel in feeling at home on the waves of life. Play is a marvelous antidote for burnout.

WRITE ON! What activities engage your playful spirit? Make a list and describe how you might infuse some play into your day. Notice how play and burnout symptoms cannot easily coexist!

_____

_____

_____

_____

_____

TRANSITIONS ❖ POWER TOOL. Your most powerful tool in any work transition process is self-assessment. Today, you'll assess your key values. Values help you make decisions during a transition. They are your guiding beliefs about how you want to work and live. Call on your values to help you with burnout.

WRITE ON! To identify your key or core values, do a web search for a core values list. Identify 5–10 key values that you live by. Which may conflict with your current work situation? Which may help with a current area of stress? What do you notice? Write, read, and reflect.

_____

_____

_____

_____

_____

_____

_____

_____

_____

_____

_____

_____

_____

_____

_____

_____

_____

_____

_____

NEUROPLASTICITY ❖ FIRING AND WIRING. Neuroscience teaches us that "neurons that fire together, wire together." Linkages that are created when neurons fire make it more likely for them to fire together in the future when activated. This helps us create new positive habits; each time you practice a habit, you strengthen the firing and wiring.

WRITE ON! What is a positive new habit that would help you combat burnout? Below your response, write down the date for two months from today. What new behaviors or thoughts might be different and better after two months of "firing and wiring"?

_____

_____

_____

_____

_____

_____

_____

_____

_____

_____

_____

_____

_____

_____

_____

_____

_____

_____

WELLNESS ❖ TAKE A HIKE. A review of studies by the Peninsula College of Medicine and Dentistry confirms that exercising outdoors provides greater benefits in mental well-being, feelings of revitalization, and commitment to continued exercise than indoor workouts alone.

WRITE ON! Search online for nearby walking or hiking trails. Or simply lace up your shoes and head out the door. Before you leave and after you get back, write down three feeling words (see Week 6, Day 2). Compare the word sets. Is outdoor exercise a viable burnout reduction strategy for you?

DATE _____

SIMPLICITY ❖ THIS SEASON. You have multiple interests. There are many causes you care about. You might have a huge backlog of projects. But you can't possibly do everything all at once. As you travel through the year, it's helpful to give each season an overarching theme to guide you as you discern where to say "yes" and "no."

WRITE ON! Start with the sentence stem, "This season, my focus is . . . ," and write for five minutes. In your reflection, note any surprises or actionable ideas.

_____

_____

_____

_____

DATE _____

WEEKLY REVIEW ❖ Read back the week's entries, reflections, or both. How do you rank your burnout this week? How do you rank your satisfaction with the writing process? How is the progress of your intentions? Are you noticing changes?

On a scale of 1 (low) to 7 (high), rate your week:

Burnout?	①	②	③	④	⑤	⑥	⑦
Writing process?	①	②	③	④	⑤	⑥	⑦
Intentions?	①	②	③	④	⑤	⑥	⑦
Noticing changes?	①	②	③	④	⑤	⑥	⑦

WRITE ON! Write observations as you rate your week. Note any connections you may see.

_____

_____

_____

_____

_____

DATE _____

INTENTIONS ❖ Intention-setting involves recognizing what you want (your vision), comparing it against what's real in the present moment (current reality), and closing the gap between the two by taking intentional and manageable steps in the direction of your vision.

WRITE ON! What are three intentions for this week that will move your current reality closer to your vision?

_____

_____

_____

_____

_____

DATE _____

WELLNESS ❖ EAT YOUR SPINACH. Writing for the nutrition blog Clean Plates, certified health coach Amanda Capritto reports that dark green and leafy veggies contain folic acid, which boosts your serotonin and can protect against the negative effects of stress and burnout.

WRITE ON! What are some of your favorite veggies? Your least favorite? Make a quick list. How might you hide healthy non-faves in smoothies, stews, or casseroles?

_____

_____

_____

_____

_____

_____

_____

TRANSITIONS ❖ KEEPERS. You will not have to let go of everything in your work. List things you want to keep, such as your skills, values, knowledge, relationships, and perhaps special mementos that represent a pre-burnout time.

WRITE ON! Write about one or two things that are especially important to keep and the strengths and assets that they represent. Hold fast to these.

_____

_____

_____

_____

_____

_____

_____

_____

_____

_____

_____

_____

_____

_____

_____

_____

_____

_____

_____

_____

NEUROPLASTICITY ❖ MAKE THE POSITIVE STICKIER. Psychologist Rick Hanson describes the brain as being "Velcro for negative experiences and Teflon for positive." Because the brain is in the business of ensuring your survival, it holds onto anything that might be dangerous. Meanwhile, positive experiences, such as compliments or acknowledgment for achievements, slide right off.

WRITE ON! Think of some recent times when you have deflected or downplayed a compliment or a small success. Write them down. For each item, close your eyes, think about it, and write down an acknowledgment of your accomplishment. Smile as you do this.

_____

_____

_____

_____

_____

_____

_____

_____

_____

_____

_____

_____

_____

_____

_____

_____

_____

_____

_____

SIMPLICITY ❖ A LETTER TO CLUTTER. What if you could speak directly to those stress-inducing objects, spaces, and distractions that contribute to burnout? Writing a letter to the clutter is an effective way to vent, voice desired changes, and then initiate those changes.

WRITE ON! Start with "Dear Clutter . . ." and let yourself write freely. Find out what you have to say. Read your letter out loud to yourself if you feel comfortable doing so. Reflect on what you notice in the writing and the speaking or reading.

_____

_____

_____

_____

_____

_____

_____

_____

_____

_____

_____

_____

_____

_____

_____

_____

_____

_____

_____

ANIMAL WISDOM ❖ LET GO OF THE OLD. As she grows, Snake must shed her too-tight skin. The process isn't always easy or quick, but it's necessary for her to continue expanding.

WRITE ON! What are you shedding in this first quarter of burnout recovery? What beliefs or behaviors are shifting into better-feeling thoughts? How are you expanding in your new skin? Write, read, and reflect.

_____

_____

_____

_____

_____

_____

WEEKLY REVIEW ❖ Read back the week's entries, reflections, or both. How do you rank your burnout this week? How do you rank your satisfaction with the writing process? How is the progress of your intentions? Are you noticing changes?

On a scale of 1 (low) to 7 (high), rate your week:

Burnout?	①	②	③	④	⑤	⑥	⑦
Writing process?	①	②	③	④	⑤	⑥	⑦
Intentions?	①	②	③	④	⑤	⑥	⑦
Noticing changes?	①	②	③	④	⑤	⑥	⑦

WRITE ON! Write observations as you rate your week. Note any connections you may see.

_____

_____

_____

_____

_____

INTENTIONS ❖ Most weeks, one or more of your intentions is likely to support at least one of the four pillars of well-being: awareness, connection, insight, purpose.

WRITE ON! What are three intentions for this week? Note, if you can, which of the pillars these intentions support. Think of this higher purpose this week as you work with your intentions. Here's an example: "As I write the newsletter this week, I support the pillars of Connection and Purpose, two keys to my well-being."

_____

_____

_____

_____

_____

JOURNAL ❖ **WHY WRITING WORKS: IMMEDIACY.** Your journal is available when looping thoughts keep you up at night, just before a performance review, or in the middle of a stress attack. Its immediacy offers you much-needed control and helps you calm down.

WRITE ON! What factors of burnout are most predictably problematic for you? How might your journal's immediacy and availability support you in these times?

_____

_____

_____

_____

_____

_____

DATE _____

TRANSITIONS ❖ BEYOND THE BOX. Burnout can often make you feel boxed in, so expand that box. Remember that the burnout box is only temporary.

WRITE ON! How can you kick out one of the walls of the box? What help might you need to manifest this change? Can you meet regularly with a mentor, coach, or trusted friend? Can you shift your work hours? Reflect on your next steps.

_____

_____

_____

_____

_____

_____

_____

_____

_____

_____

_____

_____

_____

_____

_____

_____

_____

_____

_____

_____

_____

NEUROPLASTICITY ❖ CLUSTERING BEAUTY. Under stress, it's easy to lose track of the healing presence of everyday beauty. Just as you can name challenges to tame them (see Week 4, Day 4), you can name something positive to claim it.

WRITE ON! Use clustering (see Week 8, Day 2) with "Everyday beauty" as the central concept. What do you notice when you name and claim the beauty around you?

_____

_____

_____

_____

_____

_____

_____

_____

_____

_____

_____

_____

_____

_____

_____

_____

_____

_____

SIMPLICITY ❖ A LETTER FROM CLUTTER. Invite your clutter to speak directly to you. This can open a doorway to fresh perspectives and guidance, even if you feel like you are just "making it up."

WRITE ON! Revisit last week's letter to clutter. Then write "Dear (your name)" and respond as your clutter. Read what clutter has to say, out loud if possible, and write a brief reflection. Are there any surprises?

_____

_____

_____

_____

_____

_____

_____

_____

_____

_____

_____

_____

_____

_____

_____

_____

_____

_____

_____

_____

_____

_____

_____

ANIMAL WISDOM ❖ STAND ON YOUR HEAD. Ostrich is a flightless bird and thus nests underground. When she "buries her head in the sand," it's not from fear of confrontation, as is popularly believed. Rather, she's looking down into her nest to check on her eggs. What looks like avoidance is actually incubation.

WRITE ON! Sometimes we must turn things on their heads to get a fresh perspective. Is there something today that feels like avoidance? What if it is really incubation? Today, muse on that in your journal. Perhaps you'll turn your book upside-down!

_____

_____

_____

_____

WEEKLY REVIEW ❖ Read back the week's entries, reflections, or both. How do you rank your burnout this week? How do you rank your satisfaction with the writing process? How is the progress of your intentions? Are you noticing changes?

On a scale of 1 (low) to 7 (high), rate your week:

Burnout?	①	②	③	④	⑤	⑥	⑦
Writing process?	①	②	③	④	⑤	⑥	⑦
Intentions?	①	②	③	④	⑤	⑥	⑦
Noticing changes?	①	②	③	④	⑤	⑥	⑦

WRITE ON! Write observations as you rate your week. Note any connections you may see.

_____

_____

_____

_____

INTENTIONS ❖ Remember that intentions represent the outcome that we desire as well as the positive feeling that will emanate from the outcome.

WRITE ON! What are three intentions for this week? Add the feeling you will experience when the intention is manifested.

_____

_____

_____

_____

_____

_____

_____

JOURNAL ❖ CHARACTER SKETCH. A written portrait of another person, an aspect of yourself, a mood or quality or emotion—versatility is one the benefits of character sketches. A character sketch creates a fun and useful metaphor that can help you manage burnout.

WRITE ON! Choose a helpful quality. Close your eyes and imagine this quality as a person or perhaps a magical being. What does it look like? Wear? Eat for breakfast? What does it want? How can it help you with burnout recovery?

_____

_____

_____

_____

_____

_____

TRANSITIONS ❖ CHECK YOUR PROGRESS. At Week 7, Day 3, you listed what you will let go of. As we move into the "messy middle" transition stage, you will complete another assessment of your letting-go stage.

WRITE ON! Divide a page into three columns. In the first, list what you know you want to release. In the middle, list what you want to keep. In the third column, list and mark with a question what you aren't sure of. Return to the first column and check what you've ended or started to release. Where do you see your progress?

_____

_____

_____

_____

_____

_____

_____

_____

_____

_____

_____

_____

_____

_____

_____

_____

_____

NEUROPLASTICITY ❖ THE BRAIN LOVES REPETITION. Just as a pail of water creates rivulets in a hill of sand and deepens and widens existing ones, the brain loves repetition. Repetition helps install new thoughts and behaviors. Written repetition can induce a meditative state that helps the brain take in the warmth of positive self-talk.

WRITE ON! Choose a one-sentence inspirational quote, line of poetry, verse from a sacred text, saying from an elder—or make up your own. Write it ten times—by itself the first three times and with another sentence about its meaning to you after that. Read and reflect.

WELLNESS ❖ PERK UP TO THE POSITIVES. In a recent study of nurses, those who logged three positive things at least twice weekly scored lower on measures of exhaustion compared to a control group.

WRITE ON! Name three positives you notice in your life right now. These can be small (pleasant weather) or big (health or family). Pick another time this week and repeat this practice. Might this be a habit worth sustaining? Reflect.

_____

_____

_____

_____

_____

_____

_____

_____

_____

_____

_____

_____

_____

_____

_____

_____

_____

_____

_____

_____

DATE _____

ANIMAL WISDOM ❖ TENDER LOVING CARE. To many people, Deer epitomizes gentleness and tenderness. A peaceful herbivore, Deer is quiet and shy, seeking shady shelter to rest most of the day. These serene habits can be models for your own burnout recovery.

WRITE ON! When we're beset by deadlines and stressors, we're often inclined to push forward harder. Tune in to Deer's soft message today and write about ways you can offer yourself some TLC instead. Read and reflect.

_____

_____

_____

_____

_____

DATE _____

WEEKLY REVIEW ❖ Read back the week's entries, reflections, or both. How do you rank your burnout this week? How do you rank your satisfaction with the writing process? How is the progress of your intentions? Are you noticing changes?

On a scale of 1 (low) to 7 (high), rate your week:

Burnout?	①	②	③	④	⑤	⑥	⑦
Writing process?	①	②	③	④	⑤	⑥	⑦
Intentions?	①	②	③	④	⑤	⑥	⑦
Noticing changes?	①	②	③	④	⑤	⑥	⑦

WRITE ON! Write observations as you rate your week. Note any connections you may see. Look back over the last four weeks and compare your ratings. Are you noticing progress?

_____

_____

_____

_____

REVIEW ✦ INTENTIONS. In this quarter, you've set intentions every week. You've been working on breaking big goals or intentions into week-sized bites.

WRITE ON! Write about what you have learned from setting intentions each week. Are you adjusting how you craft your intentions as you go, letting yourself learn from experience? Are you discovering what a reasonable weekly intention looks like?

_____

_____

_____

_____

_____

_____

REVIEW ✦ WRITING PROCESS. You have been offered thirteen weeks of daily writing prompts. How have they supported your burnout recovery?

WRITE ON! Reflect on the usefulness of writing as a tool for self-understanding and personal recovery over this first quarter.

_____

_____

_____

_____

_____

_____

_____

_____

REVIEW ❖ THE WEAVE OF PROMPTS. This journal brings together the approaches of six experts on writing for burnout recovery. The different dimensions engage the mind, body, heart, and spirit in a variety of ways.

WRITE ON! What are you learning from the way the voices and specialties are woven together? Reflect on what you have learned or reinforced from the multiple approaches to burnout recovery.

_____

_____

_____

_____

_____

_____

_____

_____

_____

_____

_____

_____

_____

_____

_____

_____

_____

_____

_____

_____

_____

_____

_____

REVIEW ❖ THE PILLARS OF WELL-BEING. How have the four pillars of well-being (awareness, connection, insight, and purpose) shown up in your burnout recovery this quarter?

WRITE ON! What is shifting for you in any of the areas? Are you noticing any changes in your thinking or process?

_____

_____

_____

_____

_____

_____

_____

_____

_____

_____

_____

_____

_____

_____

_____

_____

_____

_____

_____

_____

REVIEW ❖ CHANGES. Over the past quarter, you have been tracking your changes. These might be dramatic, like deciding to research a new career field. They might be subtle, such as noticing that you are organically waking up without the alarm.

WRITE ON! What is changing in you? What feels different and better? What have you let go of? What have you invited in? Reflect on the behavioral, mental, emotional or wellness shifts you have made over the last thirteen weeks.

_____

_____

_____

_____

_____

_____

_____

_____

_____

_____

_____

_____

_____

_____

_____

_____

_____

_____

_____

_____

_____

_____

REVIEW ❖ WEEKLY REVIEWS. How well have the weekly reviews this quarter helped you observe and track your burnout, writing, intention, and outcomes?

WRITE ON! Write about any observations or connections you have made from Week 1 until now. Reflect on any insights or surprises.

_____

_____

_____

_____

_____

_____

QUARTERLY REVIEW ❖ How is the progress of your burnout recovery across the first thirteen weeks? How do you rank your satisfaction with the writing process? How about setting intentions? Are you noticing changes?

On a scale of 1 (low) to 7 (high), rate the first quarter:

Burnout?	① ② ③ ④ ⑤ ⑥ ⑦
Writing process?	① ② ③ ④ ⑤ ⑥ ⑦
Intentions?	① ② ③ ④ ⑤ ⑥ ⑦
Noticing changes?	① ② ③ ④ ⑤ ⑥ ⑦

WRITE ON! Evaluate the past thirteen weeks. What have been your major takeaways? Where do you feel as if you're struggling or vulnerable? What have you not yet been able to put into practice? Assess your progress, remembering to be gentle with yourself.

_____

_____

_____

_____

INTENTIONS ❖ You've completed your quarterly check-in, and we're starting a fresh thirteen-week quarter. Let's start by updating your intentions!

WRITE ON! Today, write some intentions for the next quarter. Make these intentions attainable. Finish by writing two or three intentions for this week.

_____

_____

_____

_____

_____

_____

_____

_____

_____

_____

_____

_____

_____

_____

_____

_____

_____

_____

_____

_____

_____

_____

_____

JOURNAL ❖ THE BETTER-FEELING THOUGHT. Some thoughts are neutral and objective. Some are positive. Others are loaded with emotion. Burnout recovery involves learning which thoughts are associated with unpleasant or exhausting feelings, and how different thoughts could result in better feelings.

WRITE ON! What are the feelings you would like to experience? Next to each, write a thought or two that could produce the better feeling. Read back and reflect.

_____

_____

_____

_____

_____

_____

_____

_____

_____

_____

_____

_____

_____

_____

_____

_____

_____

_____

_____

TRANSITIONS ❖ THE MESSY MIDDLE. As you continue to let go, you move to the next phase of your work transition: the in-between. You're leaving the old way, but you're not yet in the new way. This stage involves fear, confusion, fatigue, detachment, curiosity, imagination, and hope. It's uncomfortable, but the messy middle could be the most important part of your transition.

WRITE ON! Bring to mind a big transition from the past. Write about the feelings, images, reactions, and events in the messy middle. What supports or structures helped? How can you tap into these past resources now?

_____

_____

_____

_____

_____

_____

NEUROPLASTICITY ❖ HOW'S THE WEATHER? A metaphor is something in the outside world that stands in for something on the inside world. Your brain loves metaphors so much that it often conflates the metaphor with an actual thought or behavior. How can you check in with yourself and discover where your attention has been? Use a metaphor.

WRITE ON! For a simple, fast metaphoric check-in, try an internal weather report. Write and reflect using these sentence stems: *My internal weather report is ____ because ____.* Are you experiencing sunny skies or stormy seas? Frozen solid or struck by inspirational lightning?

_____

_____

_____

_____

_____

SIMPLICITY ❖ ADJUSTING YOUR FOCUS. Too much to track and too few resources? You may need a focus adjustment. This practice helps you build awareness, one of the four pillars of well-being.

WRITE ON! As we enter a new quarter, list everything that needs your attention. Then zoom in. Focus on one thing and identify the next step. Or tune inward, quiet your mind, and listen to discover what's most important. Write what you think, feel, or hear. If you prefer, start with *It may be time to readjust my focus*. Read and reflect, highlighting any clarity that came through.

_____

_____

_____

_____

_____

_____

_____

_____

_____

_____

_____

_____

_____

_____

_____

_____

_____

_____

_____

ANIMAL WISDOM ❖ TAKE A CLEARER LOOK. A night hunter, Owl is at home in darkness. His ability to see through blackness and fog helps him detect deception and trickery.

WRITE ON! Mental and physical overwhelm can rob you of clarity and make it difficult to see through the fog. Expand on yesterday's focus adjustment. What might be causing you to feel "in the dark?" Call on Owl's discernment and take a closer look. What do you need to know? How can you break through this fog? Write and reflect.

_____

_____

_____

_____

_____

WEEKLY REVIEW ❖ Read back the week's entries, reflections, or both. How do you rank your burnout this week? How do you rank your use of these writing processes? How is the progress of your intentions? Are you noticing changes?

On a scale of 1 (low) to 7 (high), rate your week:

Burnout?	①	②	③	④	⑤	⑥	⑦
Writing process?	①	②	③	④	⑤	⑥	⑦
Intentions?	①	②	③	④	⑤	⑥	⑦
Noticing changes?	①	②	③	④	⑤	⑥	⑦

WRITE ON! Write observations as you rate your week. Note any connections you may see.

_____

_____

_____

_____

INTENTIONS ❖ Intentions stick better when you frame them in positive language. Specify what you want rather than what you want to avoid. It can be surprisingly hard to not write in the negative, so if you slip up, don't worry. Just notice it, change it, and move on.

WRITE ON! What are three intentions for this week? Practice writing them in positive language, such as "I intend to plan and manage my time" rather than "I intend to stop wasting time."

_____

_____

_____

_____

_____

_____

SIMPLICITY ❖ HERE AND NOW. When life stressors increase, every possible future disaster might loom before you. Although it's reasonable to plan ahead, crowding your mind with worries drains energy and creates unhelpful mental clutter. Counteract with regular small practices of being present.

WRITE ON! Take three deep, slow breaths. Then begin a write with "In this present moment, I am noticing . . ." Explore the here-and-now, inside and out, using all your senses, for five minutes. Then read back and reflect on how it felt to explore the present moment. How would you like to carry this awareness forward?

_____

_____

_____

_____

_____

_____

TRANSITIONS ❖ FIND YOUR METAPHOR. One strategy for understanding the in-between stage of your work transition is comparing it to something familiar. Choosing a metaphor (see Week 14, Day 4) can show you what you are feeling.

WRITE ON! Think about your reactions to the in-between stage of a past or current work transition. What metaphor symbolizes your experience? Your in-between stage might feel like a roller coaster ride, planting a garden, walking through a dark forest, or putting together a puzzle. Find your metaphor, then write about what it reveals about this or a past work transition.

_____

_____

_____

_____

_____

_____

_____

_____

_____

_____

_____

_____

_____

_____

_____

_____

_____

_____

_____

_____

NEUROPLASTICITY ❖ HEIGHTENED AND FLEXIBLE AWARENESS. Dahl, Wilson-Mendenhall, and Davidson use the term *awareness* to refer to a heightened and flexible attentiveness, including mindfulness of where you are, who you are with, what you are doing, and your own internal states of mood, bodily cues, and distractions.

WRITE ON! What is the role of distraction in your life? Make a list of all the things—phone beeps, pop-ups, news feeds, online games, social media notifications—that interrupt your flexible attentiveness. How might you curb these distractions?

_____

_____

_____

_____

_____

_____

_____

_____

_____

_____

_____

_____

_____

_____

_____

_____

_____

_____

_____

_____

ANIMAL WISDOM ❖ MAKE A STINK. Nobody bothers Skunk when she turns to face them and stomps her feet. A little warning and a reputation for great upset gets everyone's attention fast! When you're feeling burned out, consider who or what you want to say no to.

WRITE ON! List all the people, places, things, or distractions you're willing to say no to. Add a checkmark next to the things you have the power to resolve or negotiate. Make a plan to negotiate with yourself or another person, keeping tact and an openness to creative problem-solving in foreground.

_____

_____

_____

_____

_____

_____

_____

_____

_____

_____

_____

_____

_____

_____

_____

_____

_____

_____

_____

_____

WELLNESS ❖ ROLE OVER. Our lives are comprised of roles: parent, employee, boss, partner, caregiver. Roles can also describe what we enjoy: runner, baker, reader, gardener. Role fatigue, which results from spending too much time or focus in one role and not enough in others, can contribute to burnout.

WRITE ON! List ten of your life roles. Mark the ones that you associate with role fatigue. Of the remaining, which could use more focus? Describe how you could create more life balance by activating a dormant role.

_____

_____

_____

_____

_____

WEEKLY REVIEW ❖ Read back the week's entries, reflections, or both. How do you rank your burnout this week? How do you rank your use of these writing processes? How is the progress of your intentions? Are you noticing changes?

On a scale of 1 (low) to 7 (high), rate your week:

Burnout?	①	②	③	④	⑤	⑥	⑦
Writing process?	①	②	③	④	⑤	⑥	⑦
Intentions?	①	②	③	④	⑤	⑥	⑦
Noticing changes?	①	②	③	④	⑤	⑥	⑦

WRITE ON! Write observations as you rate your week. Note any connections you may see.

_____

_____

_____

_____

INTENTIONS ❖ Are you making progress on your intentions? About now, you may be noticing that your intentions seem to be building on each other from week to week. This is an excellent way to map progress toward larger goals and intentions.

WRITE ON! What are three intentions for this week? These can be related to any area of your life. Break larger intentions into week-sized bites.

_____

_____

_____

_____

_____

_____

_____

JOURNAL ❖ **BEHAVIORAL REHEARSAL.** The journal can be a magic time machine in which you transport yourself into a difficult situation and try out different ways to resolve it. In cognitive therapy, this process is called a behavioral rehearsal.

WRITE ON! Write a near-future scenario that is likely to be stress-inducing— maybe a presentation, a phone call, or a job interview. Starting with the successful end in mind, write two different stories of how you got to a happy ending. Then rehearse these endings mentally, imagining yourself engaged first in the preparation, then enjoying its successful outcome. Reflect.

_____

_____

_____

_____

_____

_____

TRANSITIONS ❖ WILD THOUGHTS. While the in-between challenges you, it also offers you gifts. You are shifting the old structure and dismantling old habits and roles. You have more space for new possibilities. If you are going to change your job or leave your career, imagine possibilities. Let the wild thoughts flow.

WRITE ON! If you could create the work you would love to do, what would it be? Maybe your current work needs a different shape or setting. What in your best and wildest dreams might happen?

_____

_____

_____

_____

_____

_____

_____

_____

_____

_____

_____

_____

_____

_____

_____

_____

_____

NEUROPLASTICITY ❖ THE IMPORTANCE OF CONNECTION. Connection, the second pillar of well-being, is an important determinant in physical health. According to the research of Dahl, Wilson-Mendenhall, and Davidson, positive social connections "serve as a buffer against . . . anxiety and depression," while poor social relationships "can be more harmful than excessive drinking or smoking." Appreciation and gratitude turbo-charge the power of social relationships.

WRITE ON! Write a thank-you note to someone you feel connected to. Express your appreciation for that person's role in your life. Can you share or deliver this gift of appreciation? (Even if you don't, you will reap positive results!)

_____

_____

_____

_____

_____

_____

_____

_____

_____

_____

_____

_____

_____

_____

_____

_____

WELLNESS ❖ FIVE WORDS FOR CHANGE. According to the International Churchill Society, Winston Churchill did not coin the phrase "Keep calm and carry on." Still, the circulation of these five simple words, discovered in a London bookstore in the 1990s, has brought resilience to many over the past few decades.

WRITE ON! Reflect briefly on some of the recent challenges you have had. Create a five-word slogan that provides a positive or hopeful instruction. If you get stuck, start with this template: "Keep calm and ____ ____," "Keep ____ and carry on," or "Keep ____ and ____ ____."

_____

_____

_____

_____

_____

_____

_____

_____

_____

_____

_____

_____

_____

_____

_____

_____

_____

_____

_____

_____

ANIMAL WISDOM ❖ SCHEDULE A TIME-OUT. Sometimes, the best strategy for burnout recovery is a good time-out. Opossum outwits an enemy by "playing dead." This approach can also help delay having to make a quick decision under pressure.

WRITE ON! How might you "play Possum" for a burnout break? Schedule a nap, a long walk, or some time alone in another room or even your car. Let your mind imagine a place and planned time when you can withdraw from everything and just relax alone. Write and reflect about your break.

_____

_____

_____

_____

_____

_____

WEEKLY REVIEW ❖ Read back the week's entries, reflections, or both. How do you rank your burnout this week? How do you rank your use of these writing processes? How is the progress of your intentions? Are you noticing changes?

On a scale of 1 (low) to 7 (high), rate your week:

Burnout?	①	②	③	④	⑤	⑥	⑦
Writing process?	①	②	③	④	⑤	⑥	⑦
Intentions?	①	②	③	④	⑤	⑥	⑦
Noticing changes?	①	②	③	④	⑤	⑥	⑦

WRITE ON! Write observations as you rate your week. Note any connections you may see. Look back over the last four weeks and compare your ratings. Are you noticing progress?

_____

_____

_____

_____

INTENTIONS ❖ Intentions not only help you focus your awareness but also support the other three pillars of well-being (connection, insight, purpose) as well. Is there one or more of the pillars that has not been as present as the others in your intentions? If so, this week you may want to create an intention specifically for that pillar.

WRITE ON! Write three intentions for this week. Consider including at least one that focuses on connection, insight, or purpose.

_____

_____

_____

_____

_____

JOURNAL ❖ **WHY WRITING WORKS: ACCEPTANCE.** As one journal writer said, "My journal is the archetypal friend. It's always waiting for me, totally accepting, and present. I can ignore it and discount its value and it never takes offense. I never have to start over or apologize. What a gift!" Unconditional acceptance, a balm for burnout, is literally at your fingertips.

WRITE ON! Write about how it feels, or might feel, to be completely accepted, just exactly as you are.

_____

_____

_____

_____

_____

_____

_____

_____

TRANSITIONS ❖ SUPER SUPPORTS. Earlier, you looked at the importance of transition support in burnout. You listed people and things that give you support and perspective. You may have included historical or imaginary figures. Look at your support list from Week 8, Day 3.

WRITE ON! Imagine you are going to have a day in which you get support from people (real or imaginary) from your list to help with burnout. Briefly describe this day of super support. Reflect.

_____

_____

_____

_____

_____

_____

_____

_____

_____

_____

_____

_____

_____

_____

_____

_____

_____

_____

NEUROPLASTICITY ❖ REVISITING THE REFLECTION. There is a neurological reason why reflecting after you write helps reap the maximum benefits from your writing. When you read back and reflect on what you wrote, you pull more power from your writing. This self-witnessing originates in a part of your brain different from the one you used to write. It helps you organically make meaning, which is a boon for overcoming burnout.

WRITE ON! Repeat the internal weather check exercise from Week 5, Day 4. Pay particular attention to the reflection. What do you notice?

_____

_____

_____

_____

_____

_____

_____

_____

_____

_____

_____

_____

_____

_____

_____

_____

_____

SIMPLICITY ❖ CLEARING THE LOGJAM. Like a pile of logs that block a river from flowing, a pile of deferred tasks and projects can block the energy you need to mitigate burnout. Sometimes, moving one log is enough to unblock the river. Sometimes, taking one step on a task you've been avoiding frees up focus and energy.

WRITE ON! Describe or draw the image of logs jamming your river. Give each log a name. Choose one to address. Describe one small step you could take today to unjam the river. Take the step and write about the outcome. What's next?

_____

_____

_____

_____

_____

_____

_____

_____

_____

_____

_____

_____

_____

_____

_____

_____

_____

_____

_____

_____

DATE _____

WEEK 17 • DAY 6

WELLNESS ❖ HANDS-ON. A Cedars-Sinai study showed immune and endocrine system improvements after a 45-minute Swedish massage. Some researchers say self-massage has even greater benefits, especially for those with injury or pain.

WRITE ON! Make a list of where you hold tension or stress. If you have injuries or areas of chronic pain, note which types of touch help and which hurt. If you can, take a few minutes now and try self-massage. What effects do you notice? If you prefer to work with a practitioner, where and when can you make an appointment?

_____

_____

_____

_____

_____

DATE _____

WEEK 17 • DAY 7

WEEKLY REVIEW ❖ Read back the week's entries, reflections, or both. How do you rank your burnout this week? How do you rank your use of these writing processes? How is the progress of your intentions? Are you noticing changes?

On a scale of 1 (low) to 7 (high), rate your week:

Burnout?	①	②	③	④	⑤	⑥	⑦
Writing process?	①	②	③	④	⑤	⑥	⑦
Intentions?	①	②	③	④	⑤	⑥	⑦
Noticing changes?	①	②	③	④	⑤	⑥	⑦

WRITE ON! Write observations as you rate your week. Note any connections you may see.

_____

_____

_____

_____

INTENTIONS ❖ Remember that intentions represent the outcome that you desire as well as the positive feeling that will emanate from the outcome.

WRITE ON! What are three intentions for this week? Your brain responds better to affirmative language that moves toward what you want instead of away from what you don't want.

_____

_____

_____

_____

_____

_____

_____

_____

_____

_____

_____

_____

_____

_____

_____

_____

_____

_____

_____

_____

_____

JOURNAL ❖ ALPHAPOEM. An alphapoem is a poem in which the alphabet, or a word or phrase, is written vertically down the page. Each succeeding line begins with a word starting with the next letter. They're great for capturing quick insights, and they're a fun way to play with poetry, as this alphapoem on worry demonstrates:

W hat, me worry?

O nly if I forget to

R emember that the

R aggedy old thought can

Y ield to the new, better-feeling thought!

WRITE ON! Create an alphapoem using BURNOUT or RECOVERY. Set your time to two minutes. Ready, set, go! Don't overthink this!

_____

_____

_____

_____

_____

_____

_____

_____

_____

_____

_____

_____

_____

_____

TRANSITIONS ❖ LOOK FEAR IN THE EYE. You might feel trapped by burnout yet be afraid of breaking out of your comfort zone. One of the primary functions of fear is to prevent change. Fear wants to keep you "safe."

WRITE ON! Today, have a respectful dialogue with Fear. In your journal, tell Fear you are making changes and therefore its role will change. Express your appreciation for the ways it keeps you protected, then describe the "new normal" as you banish burnout. Ask for Fear's support. In between your statements and questions, write how Fear would respond.

_____

_____

_____

_____

NEUROPLASTICITY ❖ INSIGHT AND WELL-BEING. The relationship between insight, the third pillar, and well-being is supported in studies. "Compassionate, accepting, and growth-oriented" insights about the self are associated with "lower levels of depression and anxiety, higher levels of well-being, and real-world outcomes like improved . . . performance" in academic or workplace settings.

WRITE ON! Write three negative or disempowering beliefs that you hold about yourself. Now rewrite them from a "compassionate, accepting, and growth-oriented" perspective. Say each out loud, paying attention to what happens in your body as you say them. Reflect on your findings. Practice this reframing process regularly.

_____

_____

_____

_____

_____

_____

ANIMAL WISDOM ❖ STAY CONNECTED. Whenever her web is damaged, Spider gets to work with her repairs. She connects her slim, strong strands from her own body to fashion both her home and her hunting ground. Like Spider, you can repair any tears in your social web and reconnect with purpose. Don't let burnout rob you of your most important relationships.

WRITE ON! Make a list or a draw a cluster (see Week 8, Day 2) of your important connections—personal and professional. Write about how you can strengthen any that have been threatened by your sense of overwhelm.

_____

_____

_____

_____

_____

_____

_____

_____

_____

_____

_____

_____

_____

_____

_____

_____

_____

_____

_____

DATE _____   WEEK 18 • DAY 6

SIMPLICITY ❖ ASK ONE QUESTION. Are you feeling stuck? The process of forming a question and bringing it to your journal may help you access guidance from your wise self.

WRITE ON! Write "I feel stuck with _____." Then imagine you're consulting a wise guide who will help you get unstuck. What single question will you ask? Write that question, then answer in the voice of the wise guide.

_____
_____
_____
_____
_____
_____
_____

DATE _____   WEEK 18 • DAY 7

WEEKLY REVIEW ❖ Read back the week's entries, reflections, or both. How do you rank your burnout this week? How do you rank your use of these writing processes? How is the progress of your intentions? Are you noticing changes?

On a scale of 1 (low) to 7 (high), rate your week:

Burnout?   ① ② ③ ④ ⑤ ⑥ ⑦
Writing process?   ① ② ③ ④ ⑤ ⑥ ⑦
Intentions?   ① ② ③ ④ ⑤ ⑥ ⑦
Noticing changes?   ① ② ③ ④ ⑤ ⑥ ⑦

WRITE ON! Write observations as you rate your week.

_____
_____
_____
_____
_____

INTENTIONS ❖ Now that you are in a rhythm of breaking a longer vision into week-sized intentions and carrying the vision forward week by week, reflect on your outcomes to date. Are you noticing that you're getting more done? Are you feeling proud or more self-confident? Is your larger vision moving toward manifestation?

WRITE ON! Do a five-minute check-in on the outcomes of your intentions so far. Then write three intentions for this week.

_____

_____

_____

_____

_____

JOURNAL ❖ **WHY WRITING WORKS: EXPAND CREATIVITY.** It's easy to practice writing a poem or sketching a scene in the journal because it's safe and private. This shedding of inhibitions increases flexibility with the creative process, often leading to more creative thinking and behavioral and cognitive change.

WRITE ON! What is your relationship with your creativity? Are you finding that your journal supports the creative process?

_____

_____

_____

_____

_____

_____

_____

TRANSITIONS ❖ STUCK OR PAUSING? You may worry about getting stuck in a transition—especially in the in-between stage. It's normal—and necessary—to slow down at times. Your transition is still actively in process, even when it is not front-of-mind. If you feel stuck, remind yourself that integration is likely happening beneath the surface of consciousness, even when your transition is paused.

WRITE ON! How can you be patient with yourself? What strengths will help you pause? Come back to these answers to remind yourself that something is happening beneath the surface when you reach a pause.

_____

_____

_____

_____

_____

_____

_____

_____

_____

_____

_____

_____

_____

_____

_____

_____

_____

_____

_____

NEUROPLASTICITY ❖ A STRONG SENSE OF PURPOSE. According to Dahl, Wilson-Mendenhall, and Davidson's research, the benefits of having a strong sense of purpose include more physical activity, fewer incidences of stroke and cardiovascular events, and reduced risk of death. Subjects with this stronger sense had fewer doctor visits. They even had better financial health!

WRITE ON! Recall a time when you were working with a strong sense of purpose, whether it was parenting or volunteering or a job you loved. Focus on how your body, heart, mind, and spirit responded to the fulfillment of purpose.

_____

_____

_____

_____

_____

_____

_____

_____

_____

_____

_____

_____

_____

_____

_____

_____

_____

_____

WELLNESS ❖ LAUGH YOUR CARES AWAY. The Mayo Clinic newsletter *In Depth* reports that laughter increases oxygen intake, stimulates organ function, releases endorphins, and aids in our relaxation response.

WRITE ON! Who or what makes you laugh? When in your daily routine could you enjoy these people or things more? Write a plan that you can start this week.

_____

_____

_____

_____

_____

_____

_____

_____

_____

_____

_____

_____

_____

_____

_____

_____

_____

_____

_____

_____

SIMPLICITY ❖ PERMISSION SLIP. Do you find yourself running from one task you "should" be doing to another, never stopping to refuel? You can give yourself permission to change that.

WRITE ON! Write yourself a permission slip for a small change that would make your day a little more delightful. Write another, giving yourself permission to do this often.

_____

_____

_____

_____

_____

_____

WEEKLY REVIEW ❖ Read back the week's entries, reflections, or both. How do you rank your burnout this week? How do you rank your use of these writing processes? How is the progress of your intentions? Are you noticing changes?

On a scale of 1 (low) to 7 (high), rate your week:

Burnout?	① ② ③ ④ ⑤ ⑥ ⑦
Writing process?	① ② ③ ④ ⑤ ⑥ ⑦
Intentions?	① ② ③ ④ ⑤ ⑥ ⑦
Noticing changes?	① ② ③ ④ ⑤ ⑥ ⑦

WRITE ON! Write observations as you rate your week. Note any connections you may see.

_____

_____

_____

_____

INTENTIONS ❖ Remember that weekly intentions are often small segments of larger visions. Intention-setting advances your vision by moving your current reality closer to your vision in incremental small steps.

WRITE ON! What is the larger vision you are currently working on? What are three intentions for this week that will move your current reality closer to that vision?

_____

_____

_____

_____

_____

_____

_____

JOURNAL ❖ **CAPTURED MOMENT.** A captured moment is a short, sensory-based vignette that describes an intensely positive experience. Captured moments are great for "flash-freezing" peak experiences of peace, joy, insight, and intimacy.

WRITE ON! Remember a time when you felt awake and alive, awash in positive emotion. It can be dramatic (summiting a mountain), intimate (giving the baby a bath), or everyday (coffee on the porch at sunrise). Write 7–10 minutes with lots of sensory detail. Read and reflect. How do you feel after writing?

_____

_____

_____

_____

_____

_____

DATE _____

TRANSITIONS ❖ STEPS TO SYNCHRONICITY. You know what you want in your current transition. Maybe you have talked to someone about changes, or maybe each week you explore another work opportunity. As you take these steps, you will find some happy accidents or meaningful coincidences—synchronicities—as things begin clicking together.

WRITE ON! Think about the events and people around you. Look for surprises and things that suddenly come together to help you. Has anything given you a clue that you are moving in the right direction with your burnout recovery? In a few sentences, describe a surprise or synchronicity.

_____

_____

_____

_____

_____

_____

_____

_____

_____

_____

_____

_____

_____

_____

_____

_____

_____

_____

NEUROPLASTICITY ❖ CHARACTER SKETCH OF DISTRACTION. In Week 15, Day 4, you wrote about distractions. Awareness, the new well-being habit you are cultivating, allows you to catch yourself when you are distracted, or about to be, and brings your attention back to your preferred focal point.

WRITE ON! A friendly way to learn more about your relationship with Distraction is to write a character sketch of it (see Week 12, Day 2). Get imaginative: What does Distraction wear, eat, listen to, read, watch? What does it want? What are its favorite ways to engage with you? How can Distraction get its needs met without interrupting yours?

_____
_____
_____
_____
_____
_____
_____
_____
_____
_____
_____
_____
_____
_____
_____
_____
_____

WELLNESS ❖ RE-STORY TO RESTORE. Recent studies show that caregivers who create a resilient and coherent narrative about their difficulties have lower levels of long-term caregiving stress as well as healthier leukocyte telomere length (a biomarker of aging), compared to control group counterparts, even eighteen months after the studies. This can apply even if you're not a parent or caregiver.

WRITE ON! Set a timer for five minutes. Write about a recent stressful time. At the five-minute mark, incorporate a positive or fulfilling aspect of your story. How has this experience transformed how you see yourself? What nuggets will you hold onto?

_____

_____

_____

_____

_____

_____

_____

_____

_____

_____

_____

_____

_____

_____

_____

_____

_____

ANIMAL WISDOM ❖ TAKE YOUR TIME. As he waits for his dinner to swim past, Great Blue Heron is majestic in his patience. He lets little disturb him from his regal posture of watchful poise. Like Heron, you can practice patience as an aspect of your awareness and focus on skill-building.

WRITE ON! Bring to mind a task or project that is frustrating you. Then, in a modification of the adage "This, too, will pass," write the sentence, "Other frustrations have passed, and so will this." Continue writing about how you can bring patience and resilience to the situation.

_____

_____

_____

_____

_____

WEEKLY REVIEW ❖ Read back the week's entries, reflections, or both. How do you rank your burnout this week? How do you rank your use of these writing processes? How is the progress of your intentions? Are you noticing changes?

On a scale of 1 (low) to 7 (high), rate your week:

Burnout?	①	②	③	④	⑤	⑥	⑦
Writing process?	①	②	③	④	⑤	⑥	⑦
Intentions?	①	②	③	④	⑤	⑥	⑦
Noticing changes?	①	②	③	④	⑤	⑥	⑦

WRITE ON! Write observations as you rate your week. Note any connections you may see. Look back over the last four weeks and compare your ratings. Are you noticing progress?

_____

_____

_____

_____

INTENTIONS ❖ The weekly process of setting intentions can support any of the four pillars of well-being—awareness, connection, insight, and purpose. Aligning your intentions with well-being turbocharges them and supports your burnout recovery.

WRITE ON! This week, choose one or more pillars of well-being and write intentions that would support your awareness, connection, insight, or purpose.

_____

_____

_____

_____

_____

_____

_____

JOURNAL ❖ **BETTER-FEELING THOUGHTS, REVISITED.** You might sometimes tell yourself something that results in a feeling of worry or anxiety. Remember that when you are feeling this way, you can reach for a better-feeling thought.

WRITE ON! Write down a thought that makes you feel worried or anxious. Then name the feeling you would rather be experiencing. Write down a thought that is true and would produce that feeling. Tell that thought to yourself until you start to experience the better feeling. Note your observations about this process.

_____

_____

_____

_____

_____

_____

TRANSITIONS ❖ LETTING GO—AGAIN. In Week 12, Day 3, you listed what you are letting go of and keeping in your work transition. Look at the list again. Now examine an ending that you feel you have completed.

WRITE ON! How does it feel to have let something go? Respond to this prompt: "Now that I have let go of _____, I feel _____." Continue to explore the release and what it signifies for you.

_____

_____

_____

_____

_____

_____

_____

_____

_____

_____

_____

_____

_____

_____

_____

_____

_____

_____

_____

_____

_____

DATE _____

NEUROPLASTICITY ❖ YOUR BRAIN LOVES NOVELTY. The brain loves novelty, especially happy sensory-based surprises. Get some gel sparkle pens, colored pencils, fruit-scented markers, washi tape, and precut collage words and images that you can paste on random journal pages for discovery later.

WRITE ON! Today, play with novelty in your journal and take yourself out for a writing date in the park or a coffee shop. Bring or pick up some fun writing utensils. Notice how it feels to be playful in your journal.

_____

_____

_____

_____

_____

_____

_____

_____

_____

_____

_____

_____

_____

_____

_____

_____

_____

_____

_____

ANIMAL WISDOM ❖ BURIED TREASURE EVERYWHERE. Some say Squirrel remembers everywhere he has buried his treats. Others say he's gathered so many that he's sure to find something delicious wherever he digs! Like Squirrel, you have buried treasure troves of memories that you can recall to alleviate stress and restore calm.

WRITE ON! Today list as many gratitudes as you can, thinking of all the places you've hidden the memories away. Consider blessings of seasons, places, people, events, beliefs that sustain you, values, and your own bodily senses and functions.

_____

_____

_____

_____

_____

_____

_____

_____

_____

_____

_____

_____

_____

_____

_____

_____

_____

_____

_____

_____

WELLNESS ❖ DO WHAT YOU WANT. Zen priest Dan Zigmond recommends engaging in preferred tasks for 90 minutes of every standard workday, either consecutively or broken into smaller segments. His premise is based on a Mayo Clinic study that found doctors who spent 20 percent of their time doing what they love experienced burnout 50 percent less often than control-group physicians.

WRITE ON! To start your workday, divide your task list into two columns: what you must do and what you want to do. Plan 90 minutes for your "want to" list, perhaps as rewards or motivators for completing your "have-to" list.

_____

_____

_____

_____

_____

WEEKLY REVIEW ❖ Read back the week's entries, reflections, or both. How do you rank your burnout this week? How do you rank your use of these writing processes? How is the progress of your intentions? Are you noticing changes?

On a scale of 1 (low) to 7 (high), rate your week:

Burnout?	① ② ③ ④ ⑤ ⑥ ⑦
Writing process?	① ② ③ ④ ⑤ ⑥ ⑦
Intentions?	① ② ③ ④ ⑤ ⑥ ⑦
Noticing changes?	① ② ③ ④ ⑤ ⑥ ⑦

WRITE ON! Write observations as you rate your week. Note any connections you may see.

_____

_____

_____

_____

DATE _____   WEEK 22•DAY 1

INTENTIONS ❖ Has your current reality moved closer to your vision in the last week? Every small intention you place attention to and act on closes the gap between your current reality and your vision.

WRITE ON! What are three week-sized intentions that can help you close this gap?

_____
_____
_____
_____
_____
_____
_____

DATE _____   WEEK 22•DAY 2

SIMPLICITY ❖ PRACTICE PRUNING. In gardening, pruning adds shape and structure to bushes and trees, and gives plants more breathing space. It clears away dead material and promotes growth and flowering. You can do the same with your home and schedule. Periodically pruning away the excess brings more air and light into your life, clears deadwood, and encourages new growth.

WRITE ON! What needs pruning from your life? Read and reflect on any clarity that came forward as you were writing and describe what might help you to pare down.

_____
_____
_____
_____
_____
_____
_____

TRANSITIONS ❖ DIGGING FOR GOLD. The messy middle is shifting your boundaries. This is a good time to evaluate changes you have made already. You might be communicating more clearly with coworkers or rewriting a job description. Maybe you have gone on job interviews or changed your circumstances for the better. Consider if you might go a step further and dig for a little more gold.

WRITE ON! Write about one change you have made in your work transition. Evaluate how well it is working. Write about how you can do something else to make this change more effective and lasting.

_____

_____

_____

_____

_____

_____

_____

_____

_____

_____

_____

_____

_____

_____

_____

_____

_____

_____

_____

_____

NEUROPLASTICITY ❖ SCENTS AND SENSES. Smell is the most primitive of your five senses. Odors take a direct route to the limbic or emotional system. If you can associate a scent that has a powerful positive emotion for you—even if it doesn't relate to the topic of your writing—it can deepen your brain's "wiring and firing" (see Week 9, Day 4).

WRITE ON! First, make a list of everyday scents you love, such as coffee, tea, essential oil, or shampoo. Then choose one and inhale it while writing about the positive associations that your brain makes. Reflect.

_____

_____

_____

_____

_____

_____

_____

_____

_____

_____

_____

_____

_____

_____

_____

_____

_____

_____

ANIMAL WISDOM ❖ GET MOVING. Horses are beautiful in motion. They may prefer to spend time grazing, but often they take off just for the fun of it, tossing their heads and galloping across the field. Like Horse, you can learn the joy of spontaneous movement.

WRITE ON! How might you move around your house or neighborhood? Plan a workout that includes movement at as many speeds as your body enjoys. Take yourself for a movement break, however brief, at any time!

_____

_____

_____

_____

_____

_____

_____

_____

_____

_____

_____

_____

_____

_____

_____

_____

_____

_____

WELLNESS ❖ FREE DAYS. Time management specialist Dan Sullivan says time off is not a reward but a necessity. He suggests supporting burnout recovery by planning "Free Days"—24-hour stretches without any work-related tasks or attention—before, not after, periods of high productivity. Consider planning these days in advance and protecting them just as you would a vacation.

WRITE ON! Look at your schedule for this upcoming month. When will you be most busy? Can you plan a Free Day a few days before? List non-work activities you could enjoy. Write about the emotional component of taking a Free Day.

_____

_____

_____

_____

_____

WEEKLY REVIEW ❖ Read back the week's entries, reflections, or both. How do you rank your burnout this week? How do you rank your use of these writing processes? How is the progress of your intentions? Are you noticing changes?

On a scale of 1 (low) to 7 (high), rate your week:

Burnout?	① ② ③ ④ ⑤ ⑥ ⑦
Writing process?	① ② ③ ④ ⑤ ⑥ ⑦
Intentions?	① ② ③ ④ ⑤ ⑥ ⑦
Noticing changes?	① ② ③ ④ ⑤ ⑥ ⑦

WRITE ON! Write observations as you rate your week. Note any connections you may see. Look back over the last four weeks and compare your ratings. Are you noticing progress?

_____

_____

_____

INTENTIONS ✦ By now, you are in a rhythm of breaking a longer vision into week-sized intentions and carrying the vision forward week by week.

WRITE ON! What are three intentions for this week? See if you can keep them manageable for a seven-day week.

_____

_____

_____

_____

_____

_____

_____

_____

JOURNAL ✦ JOURNAL POETRY. Journal poetry is less formal than "real" poetry. You can play with words without expectations. You can move a poem through lots of drafts. You can write a regular journal entry but break the lines in interesting places. You can start with a line or image from a favorite poem. You can write tiny 17-syllable haiku. You can write an alphapoem (see Week 18, Day 2). Have fun!

WRITE ON! Today, write any sort of a poem in your journal. Read it out loud with pride! You're a journal poet!

_____

_____

_____

_____

_____

_____

TRANSITIONS ❖ ECHO OF THE PAST. You may hear an echo from a past transition, perhaps an unmet expectation, a reminder of a career direction that you did not take, a "lost dream" of what you expected to be doing now, or the loss of a loved one. Transition echoes can bring up painful losses.

WRITE ON! Today, write about how you can soothe the pain of a transition echo. What do you need in this moment? How can you give it to yourself?

_____

_____

_____

_____

_____

_____

_____

_____

_____

_____

_____

_____

_____

_____

_____

_____

_____

_____

_____

_____

_____

NEUROPLASTICITY ❖ LIGHTING THE KINDLING. Burnout makes it hard to feel connected to others, but in these pages you can forge a sense of connection with your journal. Use it as a container to capture a moment (see Week 20, Day 2) of positive connection, one of the pillars of well-being. This articulated connection provides the kindling for a fire of positive brain change.

WRITE ON! On the movie screen of your mind, bring up a moment of genuine connection with another person. Write in detail about the connection you felt.

_____

_____

_____

_____

_____

_____

_____

_____

_____

_____

_____

_____

_____

_____

_____

_____

_____

_____

_____

_____

DATE _____

SIMPLICITY ❖ A LETTER TO TIME. We are all in relationship with time. We interact with it every hour of every day. Is time your friend or your enemy? Do you feel pressured, chased, or trapped by time? Those feelings feed burnout. Let's open channels of communication with time.

WRITE ON! Write a letter to time as if it were a character. Let it know how you feel. Tell time what's working and not working in your relationship. Suggest or announce changes. Sign off, read back, reflect.

_____

_____

_____

_____

_____

_____

_____

_____

_____

_____

_____

_____

_____

_____

_____

_____

_____

_____

_____

_____

_____

_____

ANMAL WISDOM ❖ BEFRIEND THE DARKNESS. Bear spends the long cold months of winter alone in her den, living off her stored energy and awaiting spring's return. She slumbers peacefully as life pauses and stillness prevails. Like Bear, your messy middle might include times of lengthy darkness. Follow Bear's lesson. Trust that you have what you need to get through.

WRITE ON! Think about times when you have felt alone in a cold or dark place. What brings you out of those places? What have you come to trust? How would it impact your burnout recovery if you could befriend darkness? Write and reflect.

_____

_____

_____

_____

_____

WEEKLY REVIEW ❖ Read back the week's entries, reflections, or both. How do you rank your burnout this week? How do you rank your use of these writing processes? How is the progress of your intentions? Are you noticing changes?

On a scale of 1 (low) to 7 (high), rate your week:

Burnout?	①	②	③	④	⑤	⑥	⑦
Writing process?	①	②	③	④	⑤	⑥	⑦
Intentions?	①	②	③	④	⑤	⑥	⑦
Noticing changes?	①	②	③	④	⑤	⑥	⑦

WRITE ON! Write observations as you rate your week. Note any connections you may see.

_____

_____

_____

_____

INTENTIONS ❖ Are you remembering to keep your intentions phrased in positive language? It's okay if they come out at first in negative language because you always have the power to rewrite them.

WRITE ON! What are three intentions for this week?

_____

_____

_____

_____

_____

_____

_____

SIMPLICITY ❖ **A LETTER FROM TIME.** You recently wrote a letter to time. Now let time respond. This is an opportunity to open your heart and mind to whatever comes through your pen or keyboard. This kind of "mindful pretending" can open the door to fresh perspectives and your inner wisdom.

WRITE ON! Read the letter you wrote to time last week (see Week 23, Day 5). Start with a salutation ("Dear [your name]") and write for 5–10 minutes. Read back and reflect. Are there any surprises?

_____

_____

_____

_____

_____

_____

_____

TRANSITIONS ❖ DISTANCE LEARNING. You've looked at your strengths and skills. You've let go and released. You've considered your supports and structure. With a little distance from your burnout, you have changed things in your work and may have even changed yourself.

WRITE ON! How you feel about yourself is the engine for every work transition. Write about the changes within you. After you read what you wrote, list three words describing how you feel about yourself at this moment. If this is not exactly what you would like to feel, how can you build a bridge to better-feeling thoughts?

_____

_____

_____

_____

_____

_____

_____

_____

_____

_____

_____

_____

_____

_____

_____

_____

_____

_____

_____

_____

NEUROPLASTICITY ❖ ADDING LOGS TO THE FIRE. Psychologist Rick Hanson reports that recalling a positive experience, vividly remembering the sensory cues, and focusing steadily on it for 30 seconds can enhance its capacity to serve as a resource. The effect is like adding logs to the fire that you kindled.

WRITE ON! Bring back the captured moment of connection that you wrote in Week 23, Day 4. With as much sensory detail—sights, smells, sounds, tastes, sensations—as possible, write about it again. Read back your response, then set your phone timer for 30 seconds and hold the sensory memory. Reflect.

ANIMAL WISDOM ❖ DREAM A LITTLE DREAM. Koala lives her entire life in eucalyptus trees. Some say her diet induces a trance, and that's why she sleeps so much of the time. Perhaps she is dreaming her future?

WRITE ON! Before you write today, stare into your own imagination and let yourself be entranced with a dreamy possibility for the future. Let a feeling of ease and relief flood your body as you write. Reflect.

_____

_____

_____

_____

_____

_____

_____

_____

_____

_____

_____

_____

_____

_____

_____

_____

_____

_____

_____

_____

_____

WELLNESS ✦ SINGING IN THE RAIN. The vagus nerve is the longest cranial nerve in the body. It connects the brain, heart, and gut and regulates much of the parasympathetic nervous system, which helps you stay calm and alert. Chanting, singing, humming, and even gargling provide healthy stimulation for the vagus nerve.

WRITE ON! What are some of your favorite songs? If you need inspiration, watch a video or open your streaming app and sing along! Write down three words to describe how you feel before and after you sing. What shifted? How can you keep this practice going?

_____

_____

_____

_____

WEEKLY REVIEW ✦ Read back the week's entries, reflections, or both. How do you rank your burnout this week? How do you rank your use of these writing processes? How is the progress of your intentions? Are you noticing changes?

On a scale of 1 (low) to 7 (high), rate your week:

Burnout?	① ② ③ ④ ⑤ ⑥ ⑦
Writing process?	① ② ③ ④ ⑤ ⑥ ⑦
Intentions?	① ② ③ ④ ⑤ ⑥ ⑦
Noticing changes?	① ② ③ ④ ⑤ ⑥ ⑦

WRITE ON! Write observations as you rate your week. Note any connections you may see. Look back over the last four weeks and compare your ratings. Are you noticing progress?

_____

_____

_____

_____

INTENTIONS ❖ Review your last several weeks of intentions, along with the quarterly intention you might have set in Week 14, Day 1. How are you progressing? Is your current reality closer to meeting your vision?

WRITE ON! Set three intentions for this week. You may want to include updates to any incomplete intentions.

_____

_____

_____

_____

_____

_____

JOURNAL* WHY WRITING WORKS: EMOTIONAL MANAGEMENT. The important work of burnout recovery brings with it a host of perfectly normal, if difficult, feelings. Your journal absorbs these feelings without judgment, censure, or reprisal. As a bonus, your catharsis often brings clarity and insight.

WRITE ON! What feeling is the most difficult for you to experience during this time of burnout recovery? So far, has writing in this journal helped you manage that feeling? Do you read and reflect? If so, how has that influenced your ability to manage your feelings more mindfully?

_____

_____

_____

_____

_____

_____

TRANSITIONS ❖ COME TO YOUR SENSES. Your five senses help you become more creative about your work transition. Right now, focus on something you see, hear, touch, taste, or smell that gives you pleasure. Recall a particular song, sound, texture, flavor, or scent. When you feel the pull of burnout, how can this sensory experience give you a boost?

WRITE ON! Capture a sensory experience that you can vividly recall. Bring it to mind when you need a boost of energy or soothing.

_____

_____

_____

_____

_____

_____

_____

_____

_____

_____

_____

_____

_____

_____

_____

_____

_____

_____

_____

NEUROPLASTICITY ❖ TAKING IN THE WARMTH. On Week 23, Day 4, we've followed Rick Hanson's process of kindling a fire and throwing on a log. The last step is to take in its warmth.

WRITE ON! Return to your captured moment from Week 23, Day 4 and allow yourself to bask in it. Write about this experience of connection again. Really enjoy the feelings of intimacy, friendship, or respect. How did it feel in your core? What does it mean to you to have had that savored experience? Reflect.

_____

_____

_____

_____

_____

_____

_____

_____

_____

_____

_____

_____

_____

_____

_____

_____

_____

_____

_____

_____

WELLNESS ❖ SLEEP ON IT. According to a study from the *Journal of Occupational Health Psychology,* the main factor in burnout development was "too little sleep," defined as less than six hours average per night.

WRITE ON! List some of the things that keep you up late or wake you early. Choose two items from your list. Give yourself some advice about how to reduce these stressors. Notice if your sleep improves.

SIMPLICITY ❖ CHUNKING YOUR DAY. It can be helpful to group similar tasks together in your schedule. Grouping similar activities together can help your day feel more intentional and less random.

WRITE ON! Start by writing "Today I'm going to put like things together in my schedule." Explore this idea, then read and reflect.

_____

_____

_____

_____

_____

_____

WEEKLY REVIEW ❖ Read back the week's entries, reflections, or both. How do you rank your burnout this week? How do you rank your use of these writing processes? How is the progress of your intentions? Are you noticing changes?

On a scale of 1 (low) to 7 (high), rate your week:

Burnout?	①	②	③	④	⑤	⑥	⑦
Writing process?	①	②	③	④	⑤	⑥	⑦
Intentions?	①	②	③	④	⑤	⑥	⑦
Noticing changes?	①	②	③	④	⑤	⑥	⑦

WRITE ON! Write observations as you rate your week. Note any connections you may see.

_____

_____

_____

_____

_____

REVIEW ❖ INTENTIONS. In this quarter, you've continued setting intentions for your week. You've been working on breaking big goals or intentions into week-sized bites. You learned strategies to make intention-setting more purposeful.

WRITE ON! Write about what you have learned from setting intentions each week. Are you noticing that they assist you in working with purpose? If you are regularly meeting most or all of your intentions, do you notice any shifts in how you see yourself, such as feeling more confident or courageous? Write and reflect.

_____

_____

_____

_____

_____

REVIEW ❖ WRITING PROCESS. How did the daily or near-daily writing work for you in the second quarter? Are you finding your own rhythm and pattern of writing? Are you gaining useful insights in your reflection writing?

WRITE ON! Reflect on the usefulness of writing and reflecting as tools for self-understanding and personal recovery over this quarter.

_____

_____

_____

_____

_____

_____

_____

_____

REVIEW ❖ THE WEAVE OF PROMPTS. Are any prompt categories particularly useful for you? What are you learning from the way the voices and specialties are woven together?

WRITE ON! Reflect on the categories of prompts that have been most useful for you this quarter.

_____

_____

_____

_____

_____

_____

_____

_____

_____

_____

_____

_____

_____

_____

_____

_____

_____

_____

REVIEW ❖ THE PILLARS OF WELL-BEING. How have the four pillars of well-being (awareness, connection, insight, and purpose) shown up in your life this quarter?

WRITE ON! What is shifting for you in any of the areas of awareness, connection, insight, and purpose? Are you noticing changes in your thinking or process? Write and reflect.

_____

_____

_____

_____

_____

_____

_____

_____

_____

_____

_____

_____

_____

_____

_____

_____

_____

_____

_____

_____

_____

_____

REVIEW ❖ CHANGES. What are you noticing about shifts and changes as you review this quarter? What is different and better?

WRITE ON! What has started to shift in your thinking, feeling, and doing that has made things different and better than they were at the start of this quarter? What have you let go of? What have you invited in? Reflect on the behavioral, mental, emotional, or wellness changes you have noticed over the last thirteen weeks.

_____

_____

_____

_____

_____

_____

_____

_____

_____

_____

_____

_____

_____

_____

_____

_____

_____

_____

_____

REVIEW ❖ WEEKLY REVIEWS. How well have the weekly reviews this quarter helped you observe and track your burnout, writing, intention, and outcomes?

WRITE ON! Write about any observations or correlations you have made in the last thirteen weeks. Compare your notes to those from Week 13. Reflect on any insights or surprises.

_____

_____

_____

_____

_____

QUARTERLY REVIEW ❖ We are at the halfway point of this journal. Looking back on the last three months, how would you summarize your progress? Where are you now in your burnout recovery program?

On a scale of 1 (low) to 7 (high), rate the second quarter:

Burnout?	①	②	③	④	⑤	⑥	⑦
Writing process?	①	②	③	④	⑤	⑥	⑦
Intentions?	①	②	③	④	⑤	⑥	⑦
Noticing changes?	①	②	③	④	⑤	⑥	⑦

WRITE ON! Evaluate the past thirteen weeks. What have been your major takeaways? Where do you feel as if you're struggling or vulnerable? What have you not yet been able to put into practice? Assess your progress, remembering to be gentle with yourself.

_____

_____

_____

_____

INTENTIONS ❖ You've completed your quarterly check-in, and we're starting a fresh twelve-week quarter. Let's start by updating your intentions!

WRITE ON! Today, write some intentions for the next quarter. Make these intentions attainable. Finish by writing two or three intentions for this week.

_____

_____

_____

_____

_____

_____

_____

_____

_____

_____

_____

_____

_____

_____

_____

_____

_____

_____

_____

_____

_____

_____

JOURNAL ❖ WHY WRITING WORKS: TRACKING CYCLES AND PATTERNS. Our habituated behaviors either promote wellness or contribute to discomfort. When you write, you create a behavioral database that can be used to track trends toward wellness or burnout.

WRITE ON! In the writing you've done in the past six months, have you started noticing cycles and patterns? Are there predictable stimuli that set off a particular burnout reaction? Or are you noticing that one shift is making a difference and creating a new pattern?

_____

_____

_____

_____

_____

_____

_____

_____

_____

_____

_____

_____

_____

_____

_____

_____

_____

_____

TRANSITIONS ❖ PINGING TRANSITIONS. As you manage work burnout, you may be undergoing other transitions that activate or amplify each other. Changes in finances, relationships, or housing can "ping" against your burnout transition. Focusing first on the most important transition helps you handle the others.

WRITE ON! Write and circle "My Burnout" in the middle of a page. Draw an arrow from the center circle, add another circle, and write the name of another transition inside. Continue adding arrows and circles; your finished drawing will look like spokes on a wheel. Reflect on what you see. Where is most of your energy going? Do you see how this pinging is affecting you?

_____

_____

_____

_____

_____

NEUROPLASTICITY ❖ MINDFUL BREATHING. According to research by psychologist Richard Davidson, bringing mindfulness to breathing soothes and calms overactive nervous systems. Among the benefits are improved focus, memory, listening skills, and engagement. To practice, bring full attention to inhaling for four counts, holding your breath for four counts, and then exhaling for seven counts. Keep the exhales longer than the inhales for maximum benefit.

WRITE ON! Try using this breathwork technique for three minutes with your eyes closed. Then write for three minutes about how you feel after. Repeat as needed.

_____

_____

_____

_____

SIMPLICITY ❖ GOOD ENOUGH. The need to do everything perfectly can contribute to burnout by leaving you feeling overwhelmed or wanting to procrastinate or avoid a task. For many tasks, it's fine to aim for an outcome that is "good enough," instead of perfect.

WRITE ON! Choose a project that feels overwhelming because of what it will take to do it perfectly or "right." Write for five minutes, starting with the prompt: "If I let myself do a 'good enough' job . . ." Reflect.

_____

_____

_____

_____

_____

_____

_____

_____

_____

_____

_____

_____

_____

_____

_____

_____

_____

_____

_____

WELLNESS ❖ A BALANCED VIEW. In 1976, Bill Hettler, cofounder of the National Wellness Institute, developed the first "wellness wheel," a circular diagram divided into six wedges, each representing one of these these life areas: physical, social, intellectual, spiritual, emotional, and occupational. The wheel shows how wellness can be cultivated across all life areas.

WRITE ON! Draw a wellness wheel. Let its outer edge represent total satisfaction and its center point, its absence. Draw a line in each domain representing your current satisfaction level. Observe your ratings and reflect. In what areas is your satisfaction strong? What areas need work? What's your improvement plan?

_____

_____

_____

_____

WEEKLY REVIEW ❖ Read back the week's entries, reflections, or both. How do you rank your burnout this week? How do you rank your use of these writing processes? How is the progress of your intentions? Are you noticing changes?

On a scale of 1 (low) to 7 (high), rate your week:

Burnout?	①	②	③	④	⑤	⑥	⑦
Writing process?	①	②	③	④	⑤	⑥	⑦
Intentions?	①	②	③	④	⑤	⑥	⑦
Noticing changes?	①	②	③	④	⑤	⑥	⑦

WRITE ON! Write observations as you rate your week. Note any connections you may see.

_____

_____

_____

_____

_____

INTENTIONS ✦ Are your intentions helping you focus and organize your week around outcomes that advance your visions?

WRITE ON! This week, review your larger vision. How is it progressing? Are you encountering stumbling blocks? Write three intentions that will help you advance your vision or resolve a particular block or impediment.

_____

_____

_____

_____

_____

_____

_____

_____

_____

_____

_____

_____

_____

_____

_____

_____

_____

_____

_____

WELLNESS ❖ GABA-DABBA-DO! Gamma-aminobutyric acid (GABA) is a neurotransmitter that has a calming effect on the body and can come from your diet. GABA plays a powerful role in reducing anxiety and depression. GABA-rich foods include almonds, walnuts, lentils, beef, brown rice, whole oats, oranges, bananas, broccoli, and spinach.

WRITE ON! When do you tend to feel most stressed? Jot down a few specific times and circumstances. Choose two or three GABA-rich foods from the above list. Create a quick plan for making them available and easy to grab during these higher stress times.

_____
_____
_____
_____
_____
_____
_____
_____
_____
_____
_____
_____
_____
_____
_____
_____
_____
_____

TRANSITIONS ❖ ON PURPOSE. Our work must matter if we are to be fulfilled. We need a purpose. Lifting yourself from work burnout is a courageous purpose. During your transition, you also may be rediscovering purpose or finding new purpose.

WRITE ON! What is the purpose that has driven you so far in your work life? Does that purpose still drive you? Has burnout recovery pointed you in the direction of a new purpose? What is it and how might you fulfill it? Write, read back, and reflect.

_____

_____

_____

_____

NEUROPLASTICITY ❖ MINDFULNESS MEDITATION. According to psychologist and author Daniel Goleman, the areas of our brain related to attention, learning, and compassion are stronger in those who perform mindfulness meditations. Practicing these three qualities, especially through meditation, is a solid remedy for burnout.

WRITE ON! Try meditation for just a few minutes. If you're new to mindfulness meditation, read a few articles online to orient yourself. Write three feeling words (see Week 6, Day 2) before and after meditating to track its outcomes and benefits.

_____

_____

_____

_____

_____

ANIMAL WISDOM❖ THE CALM HEART OF THE WHALE. Larger than any dinosaur, Blue Whale weighs up to 180 tons (163 metric tons), with a 400-pound (181 kg) heart whose tranquil beating can be heard 2 miles (3.2 km) away. Your writing this week has already taken you into the calming rhythms of your own heart through nutrition, sensory awareness, and meditation.

WRITE ON! When are you most calm? When does your emotional heart feel large and full? Write about how you can model after Blue Whale's tranquil heart to help mitigate burnout symptoms.

_____

_____

_____

_____

_____

_____

_____

_____

_____

_____

_____

_____

_____

_____

_____

_____

_____

_____

SIMPLICITY ❖ CLEARING WORRY. Worries can crowd your head and heart. They get in the way of clear thinking and decisive action. We often worry about things outside our control while ignoring worries about things we can affect.

WRITE ON! Quickly list eight worries in the background or foreground of your mind. Circle ones that you have the power to affect. Choose any one and write an action step you could take. Don't worry about mapping out all the steps required. Just identify a first step.

_____

_____

_____

_____

_____

WEEKLY REVIEW Read back the week's entries, reflections, or both. How do you rank your burnout this week? How do you rank your use of these writing processes? How is the progress of your intentions? Are you noticing changes?

On a scale of 1 (low) to 7 (high), rate your week:

Burnout?	①	②	③	④	⑤	⑥	⑦
Writing process?	①	②	③	④	⑤	⑥	⑦
Intentions?	①	②	③	④	⑤	⑥	⑦
Noticing changes?	①	②	③	④	⑤	⑥	⑦

WRITE ON! Write observations as you rate your week. Note any connections you may see. Look back over the last four weeks and compare your ratings. Are you noticing progress?

_____

_____

_____

_____

INTENTIONS ❖ Perhaps you are noticing that setting weekly intentions brings focus and orients you toward action and productivity.

WRITE ON! Are you noticing outcomes from your intentions? Write for five minutes about how intentions are assisting your burnout recovery. Then write three intentions for this week.

_____

_____

_____

_____

_____

_____

WELLNESS ❖ LISTEN TO YOUR HEART. Buddhist teacher Jack Kornfield says our 24-hour society leaves us little time to pause in a "quiet heart." The Sabbath, he says, is not only a religious concept but also a time to pause and pay deep attention to what is important, without the interruption of daily concerns or work. Whether or not you observe a religious Sabbath, consider setting aside regular time to pause and attend to what matters to you.

WRITE ON! Today, listen to your quiet heart. Invite your heart to speak to the idea of a regular "Sabbath" time. Write what you hear.

_____

_____

_____

_____

_____

_____

TRANSITIONS ❖ INFORMATION, PLEASE. You have gathered and written about many topics related to your work transition. You're building strong roots as you approach the next step in your transition: the New Way. Are there other resources you need—professional experts, financial support, mentors, classes, or training? Look for gaps.

WRITE ON! List any additional resources and help you need. Rank these resources based on how helpful they will be. What are the best ways to access the top two or three resources? You might do some research, reach out by phone or email, or schedule a visit. By when will you act?

_____

_____

_____

_____

_____

_____

_____

_____

_____

_____

_____

_____

_____

_____

_____

_____

_____

_____

_____

_____

NEUROPLASTICITY ❖ YOUR BRAIN ON GRATITUDE. Psychologist Kelly McGonigal found that gratitude works as a powerful motivator in forming new habits. When you are thankful for even small things, you encourage yourself to pay attention to good moments and feel willing to receive them. Doing so provides powerful neurological reinforcement for changing the habits of burnout.

WRITE ON! Explore gratitude by drawing a cluster (see Week 8, Day 2) with "Gratitude" in the middle of the page, capture a moment (see Week 20, Day 2) when you experienced gratitude, or create a character sketch (see Week 12, Day 2) of gratitude.

_____

_____

_____

_____

_____

_____

_____

_____

_____

_____

_____

_____

_____

_____

_____

_____

_____

_____

_____

SIMPLICITY ❖ THE POWER OF SLOW. Are there tasks that you typically try to rush through? Do you tend to multitask? You can clear mental clutter by slowing down, breathing, and engaging in one task slowly and with presence.

WRITE ON! Think about something you typically rush through without paying attention. Engage in it for 5 to 7 minutes, tackling it slowly and with full attention. If you can't do the activity, write for 5 to 7 minutes about how you would slow it down and what it would feel like to do it at a relaxed pace. Reflect.

_____

_____

_____

_____

_____

_____

_____

_____

_____

_____

_____

_____

_____

_____

_____

_____

_____

_____

_____

ANIMAL WISDOM ❖ CUDDLE UP. No matter what, Cat will find a comfortable place to curl up for a nap. Just looking at a sleeping Cat brings a sensation of peaceful relaxation. Take a hint from Cat and take at least one thoroughly relaxing break today to mitigate your burnout.

WRITE ON! Design the perfect 15-minute break. Will you read? Eat snacks? Take a walk or a Cat nap? How can you bring more calm and peaceful relaxation into today? Describe your break and how you will feel during and after. Then take your perfect break!

_____

_____

_____

_____

_____

WEEKLY REVIEW ❖ Read back the week's entries, reflections, or both. How do you rank your burnout this week? How do you rank your use of these writing processes? How is the progress of your intentions? Are you noticing changes?

On a scale of 1 (low) to 7 (high), rate your week:

Burnout?	①	②	③	④	⑤	⑥	⑦
Writing process?	①	②	③	④	⑤	⑥	⑦
Intentions?	①	②	③	④	⑤	⑥	⑦
Noticing changes?	①	②	③	④	⑤	⑥	⑦

WRITE ON! Write observations as you rate your week. Note any connections you may see.

_____

_____

_____

_____

_____

DATE _____

INTENTIONS ❖ Now that you are more than halfway through this journal, it's a good time to look back at your intentions in the early weeks and note your progress. You can also check out the "intentions" ratings in your Day 7 entries.

WRITE ON! What do you notice about the movement of your intentions? How are they supporting a larger vision? Write for five minutes about your intentions review. Then write three intentions for this week.

_____

_____

_____

_____

_____

DATE _____

JOURNAL ❖ DIALOGUE. A journal dialogue is a written conversation in which you write both parts, like a script. It requires willingness to temporarily suspend disbelief and engage in another's thoughts and feelings. But it's often surprisingly powerful in its ability to offer awareness, insight, and connection—three pillars of well-being.

WRITE ON! Choose a dialogue partner, whether it is an actual person or a personification of an abstract idea, like burnout or relaxation. Imagine you are together in a beautiful place in nature. Have a productive, respectful conversation, asking questions and answering them in turn. Stay friendly.

_____

_____

_____

_____

_____

_____

TRANSITIONS ❖ SIDE TRIP. As you gain more resources, your work transition may take an interesting turn. You learn about an unadvertised job, a new funding program, or an unexpected offer of help. Trust your instincts and explore the possibilities. You never know where these side trips may lead, even if you cannot see an immediate application.

WRITE ON! Describe a side trip in your work transition. What were the circumstances, the people involved, and your reactions?

_____

_____

_____

_____

_____

_____

_____

_____

_____

_____

_____

_____

_____

_____

_____

_____

_____

_____

_____

_____

NEUROPLASTICITY ❖ YOUR BRAIN ON JOY. Kelly McGonigal found that positive habit formation is enhanced when you take joy in the process of creating the new behavior. The joy creates internal rewards in the form of feel-good neurotransmitters that flood your brain when you practice a new habit.

WRITE ON! Although change can be hard, look for the joy in making this investment in yourself to overcome your burnout. Reflect. How can you keep joy in the front of your mind?

_____

_____

_____

_____

_____

_____

_____

_____

_____

_____

_____

_____

_____

_____

_____

_____

_____

_____

_____

_____

ANIMAL WISDOM ❖ LOOK FOR HAPPINESS. You can count on the swift appearance of Hummingbird and her flash of color to bring a smile. However fleeting, the sight of this little creature will always lift your mood. When you feel burned out, you miss the joy that little things like Hummingbird's visit can bring.

WRITE ON! Yesterday, you wrote about how you can keep joy front-of-mind. Today, deepen this exploration by listing all the small daily comforts and pleasures that bring you joy, from a cup of chamomile tea to the walk to the mailbox. Celebrate each one!

_____

_____

_____

_____

_____

_____

_____

_____

_____

_____

_____

_____

_____

_____

_____

_____

_____

_____

_____

_____

WELLNESS ❖ PEACEFUL SPACES. According to wellness expert and mind-body researcher Esther M. Sternberg, our surroundings and home environment can enhance our health or contribute to illness. She places a jasmine tree on her deck for a fragrant and visual reminder of relaxing times in Crete.

WRITE ON! Where in your space do you spend most of your time? What can you add to this space to increase your enjoyment or relaxation? Write in the present tense using sensory words, as if you have already done this. Read back and reflect, noting any action steps to take.

_____

_____

_____

_____

WEEKLY REVIEW ❖ Read back the week's entries, reflections, or both. How do you rank your burnout this week? How do you rank your use of these writing processes? How is the progress of your intentions? Are you noticing changes?

On a scale of 1 (low) to 7 (high), rate your week:

Burnout?	①	②	③	④	⑤	⑥	⑦
Writing process?	①	②	③	④	⑤	⑥	⑦
Intentions?	①	②	③	④	⑤	⑥	⑦
Noticing changes?	①	②	③	④	⑤	⑥	⑦

WRITE ON! Write observations as you rate your week. Note any connections you may see. Look back over the last four weeks and compare your ratings. Are you noticing progress?

_____

_____

_____

_____

INTENTIONS ❖ As previously noted, some intentions are internally sourced and some are deadline-driven or otherwise externally sourced. Although internally sourced intentions are more likely to gain traction, some weeks you just need to get things done.

WRITE ON! Write three intentions for this week, paying particular attention to anything that may be carry-overs or needs to be cleared from your to-do list.

_____

_____

_____

_____

_____

_____

_____

SIMPLICITY ❖ **CONTEMPLATING SPACIOUSNESS.** Spaciousness is a precious and often undervalued commodity. Even small amounts of spaciousness can make a big difference in your home, head, heart, and schedule.

WRITE ON! Write an alphapoem (see Week 18, Day 2) using the word *spaciousness*. Remember to unhook your brain and write quickly. Take what comes. Read back the poem. To expand this work, choose any line or phrase from the poem and use it as the title of a write or the topic of another alphapoem. Reflect.

_____

_____

_____

_____

_____

_____

TRANSITIONS ❖ PERSONAL FAVORITE. In Week 6, Day 3, you described your ideal type of work. As you prepare to move further into your work transition, think about your work history and the jobs you found most enjoyable or fulfilling.

WRITE ON! Describe a job or type of work that offered enjoyment and satisfaction. What did you do? What did you take away from that experience? Hold this memory as you think about your future steps.

_____
_____
_____
_____
_____
_____
_____
_____
_____
_____
_____
_____
_____
_____
_____
_____
_____
_____
_____
_____
_____

NEUROPLASTICITY ❖ DOWN THE DRAIN. Author and neuroendocrine researcher Robert Sapolsky reports that our brain conflates the literal and the metaphorical. For instance, as you are soaping up in the shower or tub, imagine yourself feeling "cleansed" of burnout.

WRITE ON! Imagine how it would feel to soap up and rinse all that stress down the drain. What kind of stress are you washing down the drain? Then take a shower or bath—either physically or in your mind—and actively imagine yourself scrubbed clean of stress. Write about your visualization. Read back and reflect.

_____
_____
_____
_____
_____
_____
_____
_____
_____
_____
_____
_____
_____
_____
_____
_____
_____
_____

WELLNESS ❖ WRITING WHAT AILS YOU. A research team at Duke and Vanderbilt led by wellness expert John Evans offered six weeks of facilitated writing to recently traumatized outpatient participants. Compared to the control group, the writers increased their overall resilience and decreased levels of depressive symptoms, rumination, and perceived stress levels.

WRITE ON! Name a difficulty you have overcome during burnout recovery. Write about it from several perspectives. For example, make a list of ways you overcame it; write a letter to someone about the meaning of this upheaval; and create a story or journal poem about the challenge. Read and reflect.

_____

_____

_____

_____

_____

_____

_____

_____

_____

_____

_____

_____

_____

_____

_____

_____

_____

_____

_____

DATE _____

ANIMAL WISDOM❖ EXPECT GOOD FORTUNE. Depending upon its color, Koi can symbolize abundance, perseverance, prosperity, and transformation. Although small, these fish are powerful and hardy. The oldest Koi is said to be Hanako, who lived to be about 226 years old!

WRITE ON! Adopt Koi as your power animal and look ahead five years. Describe the best attainable version of your life. Be sure to note the benefits of burnout recovery on your health, love, satisfaction, and well-being.

_____

_____

_____

_____

_____

DATE _____

WEEKLY REVIEW ❖ Read back the week's entries, reflections, or both. How do you rank your burnout this week? How do you rank your use of these writing processes? How is the progress of your intentions? Are you noticing changes?

On a scale of 1 (low) to 7 (high), rate your week:

Burnout?   ① ② ③ ④ ⑤ ⑥ ⑦

Writing process? ① ② ③ ④ ⑤ ⑥ ⑦

Intentions?   ① ② ③ ④ ⑤ ⑥ ⑦

Noticing changes? ① ② ③ ④ ⑤ ⑥ ⑦

WRITE ON! Write observations as you rate your week. Note any connections you may see.

_____

_____

_____

_____

_____

INTENTIONS ❖ When setting intentions, it's useful to include the feeling that will result from realizing them. This brings in the sensory experience that deepens the neurological connection and strengthens the capacity to believe that your intentions are attainable.

WRITE ON! What are three intentions for this week? Add the feeling you will experience when you attain the intention.

_____

_____

_____

_____

_____

SIMPLICITY ❖ A SPACIOUS DRAWER. Like people, drawers require spaciousness to function well. When your drawers are crammed too full, struggling with them can add to your frustration and irritation.

WRITE ON! Focus on one overly full drawer in your kitchen, bedroom, or workspace and write or draw what is in it. Imagine transforming it so that it contains only what is needed, plus some extra room. Write about the pleasurable experience of opening that transformed drawer. Read back and reflect. Then schedule 15–20 minutes to clear that drawer.

_____

_____

_____

_____

_____

_____

_____

TRANSITIONS ❖ FITTING PIECES TOGETHER. The middle of your transition from burnout has a lot of puzzle pieces. There are some old ones you are keeping and some new ones you are creating.

WRITE ON! Describe the pieces of your new work picture that you still need. Write a few sentences about how you will find those pieces. This can be anything from having a certain kind of work area or coworkers to sharing job responsibilities. Notice how you feel as you identify those pieces.

_____

_____

_____

_____

_____

_____

_____

_____

_____

_____

_____

_____

_____

_____

_____

_____

_____

_____

_____

_____

NEUROPLASTICITY ❖ SAVOR AND CELEBRATE. Burnout recovery is rooted in small steps of progress, and savoring and celebrating progress helps make the positive experiences stick in your brain. Making note of—and writing about—successes, even small ones, supports burnout management.

WRITE ON! List several small successes you have recently experienced. Celebrate a win on the page by writing a captured moment of an item on the list. Use sensory language to describe your success.

_____

_____

_____

_____

_____

_____

_____

_____

_____

_____

_____

_____

_____

_____

_____

_____

_____

_____

_____

_____

_____

ANIMAL WISDOM ❖ FIGHT, FLIGHT, FREEZE. When threatened, all animals, including humans, instinctively choose among three responses: fight, flight, or freeze in place. Fleetfooted Rabbit is equally adept at flight and freeze.

WRITE ON! What is your default reaction to stress? Are you a fighter? Would you love to just get away from it all? Or has burnout frozen you in place? Like Rabbit, you may experience two or all three reactions.

_____

_____

_____

_____

_____

_____

_____

_____

_____

_____

_____

_____

_____

_____

_____

_____

_____

_____

_____

_____

_____

DATE _____

WELLNESS ❖ FINISH WHAT YOU STARTED. Emily and Amelia Nagoski, authors of *Burnout*, recommend "completing the stress cycle" to combat burnout. Daily stress activates our fight-flight-freeze survival response. When we aren't in real danger or don't complete this cycle by running away or standing our ground, this energy remains stuck in the nervous system. Physical activity or affection, such as a brief 20-second hug, are two of the most effective ways to provide release.

WRITE ON! Make a list of physical movements you enjoy and people or animals that provide you with comfort or affection. Schedule 10 minutes in your day to enjoy these resources.

_____

_____

_____

_____

DATE _____

WEEKLY REVIEW ❖ Read back the week's entries, reflections, or both. How do you rank your burnout this week? How do you rank your use of these writing processes? How is the progress of your intentions? Are you noticing changes?

On a scale of 1 (low) to 7 (high), rate your week:

Burnout? ① ② ③ ④ ⑤ ⑥ ⑦

Writing process? ① ② ③ ④ ⑤ ⑥ ⑦

Intentions? ① ② ③ ④ ⑤ ⑥ ⑦

Noticing changes? ① ② ③ ④ ⑤ ⑥ ⑦

WRITE ON! Write observations as you rate your week. Note any connections you may see. Look back over the last four weeks and compare your ratings. Are you noticing progress?

_____

_____

_____

_____

INTENTIONS ✦ Today, look back on the past several weeks of intentions. Are you able to track patterns and changes? Might your intentions be growing a bit stale? If so, perhaps you could freshen them.

WRITE ON! Write three intentions for this week. Include one or two new intentions if you feel yours are growing stale.

_____

_____

_____

_____

_____

_____

_____

JOURNAL ✦ **WHY WRITING WORKS: STRENGTHEN INTUITION AND INNER GUIDANCE.** Your journal becomes a bridge between you and your intuition. The "still, small voice" of your inner wisdom becomes clear as you learn to tune in, listen, ask, and act.

WRITE ON! Burnout can blunt that voice into a barely discernable whisper. Today, write about your intuitive sense or your connection to your wise self. Center yourself and become still. Ask a question. Listen for a whisper, a nudge, or a bodily sensation. Write what comes.

_____

_____

_____

_____

_____

_____

TRANSITIONS ❖ TEMPORARY ROADBLOCKS. As your work transition advances, it is normal to find roadblocks in your path. It's easier to chip away at these roadblocks because you are energized by being on your right and true path. If a family disruption, a health problem, or an unexpected deadline temporarily interferes with your transition, it's okay. You can work through these obstacles.

WRITE ON! Name or draw a roadblock you are facing now or expect to face. Write about one or two ways you can chip away at it. Remember the importance of your strengths, structures, values, and sources of support.

_____

_____

_____

_____

_____

_____

_____

_____

_____

_____

_____

_____

_____

_____

_____

_____

NEUROPLASTICITY ❖ SAVORING OTHERS' SUCCESS. Last week, we talked about savoring your own successes. Your marvelous brain also has "mirror neurons" that make it possible to take inspiration from the success of others.

WRITE ON! Think of a time when you felt genuine pride, joy, or inspiration in someone else's actions. Write about that moment, and savor what it meant to you. Read and reflect. If it's possible, share what you wrote with the person you wrote about; this will also help strengthen your connection with them and bring you a moment of joy.

_____

_____

_____

_____

_____

_____

_____

_____

_____

_____

_____

_____

_____

_____

_____

_____

_____

_____

SIMPLICITY ❖ BEING ENOUGH. Somewhere along the line, you may have internalized a message that your worth as a person was dependent on how much you accomplished in a day. Such messages can result in a pressure to constantly prove yourself. This can cause you to crowd your day with unrealistic expectations which, in turn, fuel the state of burnout.

WRITE ON! Write for five minutes, starting with the sentence stem, "If I knew I were enough . . ." Read and reflect.

_____

_____

_____

_____

_____

_____

_____

_____

_____

_____

_____

_____

_____

_____

_____

_____

_____

_____

WELLNESS ❖ SOAK YOUR HEAD. Marsha Linehan—the creator of dialectical behavior therapy (DBT) and physiological research—suggests that dipping your face in cold water, or applying a cold pack or cloth to your face, triggers something called the mammalian dive response. This in turn activates the parasympathetic nervous system and can increase relaxation levels during panic or distress.

WRITE ON! Note some activities, situations, or times of day that are particularly stressful for you. List sources of cold available in these environments. Experiment with the cold-water technique, making note of how you feel both before and after.

_____

_____

_____

_____

WEEKLY REVIEW ❖ Read back the week's entries, reflections, or both. How do you rank your burnout this week? How do you rank your use of these writing processes? How is the progress of your intentions? Are you noticing changes?

On a scale of 1 (low) to 7 (high), rate your week:

Burnout?	①	②	③	④	⑤	⑥	⑦
Writing process?	①	②	③	④	⑤	⑥	⑦
Intentions?	①	②	③	④	⑤	⑥	⑦
Noticing changes?	①	②	③	④	⑤	⑥	⑦

WRITE ON! Write observations as you rate your week. Note any connections you may see.

_____

_____

_____

_____

INTENTIONS ❖ We set intentions not only for what they represent (a met deadline, a completed project, a shift in thinking or feeling) but also for how we will feel as we move toward them.

WRITE ON! What are three intentions for this week? How will you feel as each intention is met?

_____

_____

_____

_____

_____

_____

ANIMAL WISDOM ❖ **SURRENDER TO CHANGE.** Tadpoles are one of the transformational stages in the life of Frog. Day by day, Tadpoles undergo bodily revisions that will enable them to live both in water and on land. Like Tadpole, you are also transforming. Tomorrow you move into the third stage of transition.

WRITE ON! Describe both your resistance to and acceptance of the changes that burnout recovery has offered you to date. What has occurred that helps you move more easily between differing roles, environments, and expectations?

_____

_____

_____

_____

_____

_____

TRANSITIONS ❖ THE NEW WAY. You are moving toward the last phase of your work transition: the New Way. It is a psychological acceptance of a new chapter in your life and something you want to grow into. At this stage, you look forward more often than you do backward. You may still find wisps of the old way, but you are crossing the threshold into a new routine and role.

WRITE ON! Write a few sentences about what you most want in the new or renewed work you are moving into.

_____

_____

_____

_____

_____

_____

_____

_____

_____

_____

_____

_____

_____

_____

_____

_____

_____

_____

NEUROPLASTICITY ❖ RIPPLES OF CHANGE. Not only can you help your brain benefit positively from the inspiration of others, but you, too, are an inspiration. Consider how a change that supports your well-being could ripple out and inspire others.

WRITE ON! Think about some of the positive steps you have taken lately for your burnout recovery. Who in your world might be motivated by what you have done for your own health and well-being? How are you being a role model for burnout recovery?

_____

_____

_____

_____

_____

_____

_____

_____

_____

_____

_____

_____

_____

_____

_____

_____

_____

_____

_____

SIMPLICITY ❖ A DAY WITH BREATHING ROOM. Do you tend to overestimate what you can do in a day? That's likely because you are assuming you can be productive at all times.

WRITE ON! Describe how you would like the day ahead to go. What if you could give yourself room to breathe and transition between activities while still having a productive day? How would you use those transitional times?

_____

_____

_____

_____

_____

_____

_____

_____

_____

_____

_____

_____

_____

_____

_____

_____

_____

_____

_____

_____

_____

_____

_____

WELLNESS ❖ HOPEFUL. Dan Tomasulo, positive psychology expert and author of *Learned Hopefulness*, says hope is one of the few feelings that thrives on adversity. When we desire something we don't have, or aren't sure we can do, hope kicks in. Through adjusting our goals or bringing them closer to our ability to attain them, he says, we recalibrate against disappointment.

WRITE ON! List current hopes that feel out of reach. What's out of your control? How might you revise your goal to make it more achievable? What steps would you need to take to make these changes?

_____

_____

_____

_____

_____

WEEKLY REVIEW ❖ Read back the week's entries, reflections, or both. How do you rank your burnout this week? How do you rank your use of these writing processes? How is the progress of your intentions? Are you noticing changes?

On a scale of 1 (low) to 7 (high), rate your week:

Burnout?	①	②	③	④	⑤	⑥	⑦
Writing process?	①	②	③	④	⑤	⑥	⑦
Intentions?	①	②	③	④	⑤	⑥	⑦
Noticing changes?	①	②	③	④	⑤	⑥	⑦

WRITE ON! Write observations as you rate your week. Note any connections you may see.

_____

_____

_____

_____

DATE _____

INTENTIONS ❖ Intentions will continue to give structure and meaning to your week. Are you remembering to keep them written in positive language?

WRITE ON! Write three intentions for this week.

_____

_____

_____

_____

_____

_____

_____

_____

DATE _____

JOURNAL ❖ PERSPECTIVES: TIME. Writing from the perspective of a point in the future alters your point of view by jumping time and imagining an outcome in which your vision has been actualized. This process helps bring conscious awareness to what you deeply desire and lets you map the trajectory to your realized success.

WRITE ON! Date your page six months from today. Imagine that you have reached some important markers in your burnout recovery. What were they? Who are you now? Write in first person using present tense ("I am . . .").

_____

_____

_____

_____

_____

_____

TRANSITIONS ❖ HERE'S THE PLAN. Most people who do well in the new way enter with a plan, two or three immediate goals, and some small steps forward. Use yesterday's write as a guide for today's write.

WRITE ON! Think of two goals you want to achieve as you enter the third stage of your work transition. For each of your stated goals, write small steps that you can take to achieve it. What do you notice when you read this over?

_____

_____

_____

_____

_____

_____

_____

_____

_____

_____

_____

_____

_____

_____

_____

_____

_____

_____

_____

_____

DATE _____

NEUROPLASTICITY ❖ FOCUSED MIND, HAPPY MIND. Focus is one key element of the well-being pillar of awareness. Harvard psychologists Matthew Killingsworth and Daniel Gilbert used a special "track your happiness" app and discovered that "a wandering mind is an unhappy mind."

WRITE ON! To keep your mind "happy" as you write, ground yourself using the five-senses check-in (see Week 3, Day 6), or mindful breathing (see Week 27, Day 4). Write quickly, describing your wandering mind with the sentence stem, "My mind is wandering over the landscape of ____." Then shift to "My focused mind pays attention to ____." Reflect on how you can stay focused and attentive.

SIMPLICITY ❖ SIMILAR THINGS TOGETHER. Stress and burnout may lead to pockets of chaos in your living space. Sorting random items into categories (such as keeping all mementos in their own shoebox) can make clutter feel more manageable and help you see more clearly what can be weeded out.

WRITE ON! Think about the piles and stacks stuffed with the miscellany of your life. Write, starting with the phrase, "It is time to put similar things together." Itemize and articulate what you expect to find. Will you store it? If so, how and where? What will you recycle, donate, or discard?

_____

_____

_____

_____

_____

_____

_____

_____

_____

_____

_____

_____

_____

_____

_____

_____

_____

_____

_____

DATE _____   WEEK 35 •Day 6

WELLNESS ❖ BUBBLE UP. Author and practicing Buddhist Sylvia Boorstein explains the title of her book on mindfulness meditation, *Don't Just Do Something, Sit There*. You will still need to act in many areas of your life. If you sit long enough, the right action will bubble up to the surface.

WRITE ON! Is there a dilemma that you have an impulsive need to resolve? Write your knee-jerk desire for action. Sit for a few minutes, breathing deeply. Reflect on your initial plan and note any shifts. Using the pillars of awareness, insight, and connection, write whatever bubbles up.

_____

_____

_____

_____

_____

DATE _____   **WEEK 35 •Day 7**

WEEKLY REVIEW ❖ Read back the week's entries, reflections, or both. How do you rank your burnout this week? How do you rank your use of these writing processes? How is the progress of your intentions? Are you noticing changes?

On a scale of 1 (low) to 7 (high), rate your week:

Burnout?	①	②	③	④	⑤	⑥	⑦
Writing process?	①	②	③	④	⑤	⑥	⑦
Intentions?	①	②	③	④	⑤	⑥	⑦
Noticing changes?	①	②	③	④	⑤	⑥	⑦

WRITE ON! Write observations as you rate your week. Note any connections you may see.

_____

_____

_____

_____

INTENTIONS ❖ Are there intentions from weeks ago that might benefit from a check-in?

WRITE ON! Write three intentions for this week, perhaps refreshing prior intentions from previous weeks that could use a boost.

_____

_____

_____

_____

_____

_____

_____

JOURNAL ❖ PERSPECTIVES: VOICE. Last week, you shifted perspective by jumping time. Today, shift perspective by writing in a different voice. Assuming someone else's perspective offers useful distance from your own up-close point of view and lets you see aspects of your story that have eluded you.

WRITE ON! Recall a recent moment of embarrassment, nervousness, annoyance, or other mild negative emotion. Place yourself in that scene. As if you are watching a movie unspool, write about the experience in the third-person voice of a compassionate witness. Read and reflect. Are there any surprises in this retelling?

_____

_____

_____

_____

_____

TRANSITIONS ❖ NOT THERE YET? As you step into the new way, things may not feel settled. You might have accepted forward movement, but your body and routine haven't quite made the shift. There might be gaps in what you are able to get done.

WRITE ON! As you execute your plan, note how it feels. Write about what you accomplished. If you did not take your intended steps, don't judge yourself harshly. Instead, write about what you might need in order to build a new routine.

_____

_____

_____

_____

_____

_____

_____

_____

_____

_____

_____

_____

_____

_____

_____

_____

_____

_____

_____

_____

_____

NEUROPLASTICITY ❖ INSIGHT AS KALEIDOSCOPE. Insight, the third pillar of well-being, is the capacity to observe and make interpretations about your thoughts, beliefs, and behaviors. Like kaleidoscopes with constantly shifting patterns of bright stones, your emotions, thoughts, and beliefs shape your experience and sense of self.

WRITE ON! Close your eyes and visualize a kaleidoscope's shifting patterns. Think about your own patterns. Write about one pattern that serves you and one that gets in your way. Read back your responses and reflect.

_____

_____

_____

_____

_____

_____

_____

_____

_____

_____

_____

_____

_____

_____

_____

_____

_____

_____

_____

SIMPLICITY ❖ TITLE YOUR DAY. When you feel like you're supposed to be doing everything at once, it's helpful to name a focus for the day. Is this an errand day? A family day? A tying-up-loose-ends day? Let the name of your day be a guide to focus your energy.

WRITE ON! Generate five possible titles for this day. Circle the one that feels best. Write about what you'll do on this day of focus. Later, reflect on your outcomes.

_____

_____

_____

_____

_____

_____

_____

_____

_____

_____

_____

_____

_____

_____

_____

_____

_____

_____

_____

_____

ANIMAL WISDOM ❖ BE A LOYAL PAL. You can always count on Dog to be loyal. Even when mistreated, Dog will return affection again and again. Nothing can prevent Dog from expressing love. The next time you have self-defeating thoughts or behaviors, treat yourself as Dog would—loving, accepting, loyal.

WRITE ON! Think about something that is causing you distress. Identify, if you can, the key feeling and the thought or source of the feeling. Now imagine that Dog is with you, lavishing you with unconditional affection. Write in the voice (see Week 36, Day 2) of that loving energy.

_____

_____

_____

_____

WEEKLY REVIEW ❖ Read back the week's entries, reflections, or both. How do you rank your burnout this week? How do you rank your use of these writing processes? How is the progress of your intentions? Are you noticing changes?

On a scale of 1 (low) to 7 (high), rate your week:

Burnout?	① ② ③ ④ ⑤ ⑥ ⑦
Writing process?	① ② ③ ④ ⑤ ⑥ ⑦
Intentions?	① ② ③ ④ ⑤ ⑥ ⑦
Noticing changes?	① ② ③ ④ ⑤ ⑥ ⑦

WRITE ON! Write observations as you rate your week. Note any connections you may see. Look back over the last four weeks and compare your ratings. Are you noticing progress?

_____

_____

_____

_____

INTENTIONS ❖ This week, you might think about intentions around anything you've been procrastinating on, shoving to the bottom of the list, or otherwise not finding time or attention for.

WRITE ON! What are your three intentions this week? See if you can include an intention about something you've been setting aside for a while.

_____

_____

_____

_____

_____

_____

_____

_____

ANIMAL WISDOM ❖ BE A STAR. Burnout can rob us of energy for fun, drama, or surprise. That's when we call in Peacock's energy. Peacock is never shy about showing off his magnificent tail feathers to attract attention. He puts his energy into strutting his stuff!

WRITE ON! Today, write a plan for cooking a fancy meal, dressing in colorful clothes, playing, dancing to your favorite music, or otherwise celebrating your creative flair. Be a star!

_____

_____

_____

_____

_____

_____

TRANSITIONS ❖ LETTING GO—AGAIN. You have listed what you are letting go of and keeping in your work transition (see Week 12, Day 3). Look at the list again. Now examine an ending that you feel you have completed.

WRITE ON! How does it feel to have let your chosen ending go? Explore how you felt about this release and what it signifies for you, starting with this sentence: "Now that I have let go of _____, I feel_____." Read back and reflect.

_____
_____
_____
_____
_____
_____
_____
_____
_____
_____
_____
_____
_____
_____
_____
_____
_____
_____
_____
_____
_____

NEUROPLASTICITY ❖ WHAT IF? Insight helps you challenge fixed beliefs that keep you stuck. Some fixed beliefs (such as "I'm not smart enough" or "Something terrible will happen if I mess up") are often instilled in childhood and follow us into adulthood. These beliefs likely weren't true then, and they're almost certainly not true now.

WRITE ON! Write three fixed beliefs about yourself. Challenge one of these beliefs. What if this isn't true? What else is true instead? Reflect on how this new awareness could help you mitigate an aspect of your burnout.

_____

_____

_____

_____

_____

_____

_____

_____

_____

_____

_____

_____

_____

_____

_____

_____

_____

_____

_____

_____

SIMPLICITY ❖ SETTING BOUNDARIES. You need space for your work. Are coworkers infringing? Are family members encroaching? Are you violating your own space with non-work-related items? All these conditions blur boundaries and make it difficult to assert yourself as you move into a healthier state of recovery.

WRITE ON! Write a journal dialogue (see Week 30, Day 2) with any violators of your workspace. In the dialogue, practice clearly and kindly stating your boundaries and asking that they be respected. As always, be open to surprises. Reflect on how you could ask for an actual conversation.

DATE _____   **WEEK 37 • DAY 6**

WELLNESS ❖ TALK YOURSELF OUT OF IT. In a UK and Netherlands study, researchers found that athletes who used motivational self-talk boosted their endurance performance and reduced their rates of perceived exertion compared to the control group.

WRITE ON! When you find yourself feeling tired or vulnerable, use your journal or smartphone recording feature to monitor your self-talk. Rewrite your most negative self-talk to be an affirmation of support and encouragement. Place this new thought where you will see it, perhaps above your desk, on your mirror, or as your screensaver. Note the results.

_____

_____

_____

_____

DATE _____   **WEEK 37 • DAY 7**

WEEKLY REVIEW ❖ Read back the week's entries, reflections, or both. How do you rank your burnout this week? How do you rank your use of these writing processes? How is the progress of your intentions? Are you noticing changes?

On a scale of 1 (low) to 7 (high), rate your week:

Burnout?   ① ② ③ ④ ⑤ ⑥ ⑦

Writing process?   ① ② ③ ④ ⑤ ⑥ ⑦

Intentions?   ① ② ③ ④ ⑤ ⑥ ⑦

Noticing changes?   ① ② ③ ④ ⑤ ⑥ ⑦

WRITE ON! Write observations as you rate your week. Note any connections you may see.

_____

_____

_____

_____

_____

DATE _____

INTENTIONS ❖ It's time to set intentions for the week!

WRITE ON! What are your three intentions for this week? How about setting at least one intention to treat yourself with something fun or relaxing?

_____

_____

_____

_____

_____

_____

DATE _____

SIMPLICITY ❖ **A SWEET GOODBYE.** It's sometimes hard to admit, but your workspace may not be able to hold every item you wish it could. Sometimes a beloved memento, a quality item, or a gift someone gave you ten years ago is just in the way.

WRITE ON! Write a letter of goodbye to this beloved object you've chosen to release. It's an opportunity to thank it, bless it on its way, and reclaim any memories or positive feelings it's been holding for you. Let it go and enjoy the gift of spaciousness you're giving yourself.

_____

_____

_____

_____

_____

_____

_____

TRANSITIONS ❖ WHO ARE YOU? In your work transition, you gained a deeper awareness of the signs of burnout and a deeper appreciation of work that matters to you. Step back and imagine the character that you were when you started your journal and the character you are now.

WRITE ON! Write a character sketch (see Week 12, Day 2) of the renewed you. How does your character look and act? What kind of work is your character doing?

_____

_____

_____

_____

_____

_____

_____

_____

_____

_____

_____

_____

_____

_____

_____

_____

_____

_____

_____

_____

_____

_____

NEUROPLASTICITY ❖ NEW PATTERNS. In life, change is constant. Burnout recovery is a process of seeing new arrangements and patterns emerge, sometimes subtly and sometimes all at once.

WRITE ON! What new patterns of well-being are emerging for you as we approach the fourth quarter of your burnout recovery?

_____

_____

_____

_____

_____

_____

_____

_____

_____

_____

_____

_____

_____

_____

_____

_____

_____

_____

_____

_____

ANIMAL WISDOM ❖ PLAN A WARM, FUZZY REUNION. Sheep flock together for safety and comfort. They are social and live in large groups, embodying the concept of strength in community. Sheep also embody "warm and fuzzy," as their wool is transformed into cozy sweaters, socks, and blankets.

WRITE ON! As you recover from your burnout, who will you invite to gather with you? Who will give you the warm, fuzzy feelings of friendship and community that can help restore your zest for life? Write about a gathering you might have.

_____

_____

_____

_____

_____

_____

_____

_____

_____

_____

_____

_____

_____

_____

_____

_____

_____

_____

DATE _____   right**WEEK 38 • DAY 6**

WELLNESS ❖ CHOOSE YOUR AUDIENCE. In her book, *I Thought it Was Just Me (But It Isn't)*, social science researcher Brené Brown discusses "shame resilience," the capacity to repurpose shame through assertive action. We can cultivate it, says Brown, by identifying specific triggers to feelings of unworthiness and sharing these experiences with trusted others instead of keeping them secret. Sometimes, we can only tell ourselves about them to start.

WRITE ON! List triggers for your feelings of shame, imperfection, or unworthiness. If you can, identify one or two people with whom you could share your vulnerabilities. Otherwise, can you tell your journal? Reflect.

_____

_____

_____

_____

_____

DATE _____   **WEEK 38 • DAY 7**

WEEKLY REVIEW ❖ Read back the week's entries, reflections, or both. How do you rank your burnout this week? How do you rank your use of these writing processes? How is the progress of your intentions? Are you noticing changes?

On a scale of 1 (low) to 7 (high), rate your week:

Burnout?   ① ② ③ ④ ⑤ ⑥ ⑦
Writing process?   ① ② ③ ④ ⑤ ⑥ ⑦
Intentions?   ① ② ③ ④ ⑤ ⑥ ⑦
Noticing changes?   ① ② ③ ④ ⑤ ⑥ ⑦

WRITE ON! Write observations as you rate your week. Note any connections you may see. Look back over the last four weeks and compare your ratings. Are you noticing progress?

_____

_____

_____

_____

REVIEW ❖ INTENTIONS. In this quarter, you've continued to set intentions, and it is likely that you are discovering your own way through the intention-setting process.

WRITE ON! Today, describe the process you are experiencing with intention-setting. Write about the overall impact that intentions are having on outcomes that you value. What is working? What isn't working as well? What might you shift for better outcomes?

_____

_____

_____

_____

_____

_____

REVIEW ❖ WRITING PROCESS. How is daily or near-daily writing working for you overall in this third quarter? Are you finding your own rhythm and pattern of writing? Are you gaining useful synthesis in the reflection writes?

WRITE ON! Reflect on the usefulness of writing and reflecting as tools for self-understanding and personal recovery over this quarter.

_____

_____

_____

_____

_____

_____

_____

_____

REVIEW ❖ THE WEAVE OF PROMPTS. Are you noticing that there are prompt categories that were particularly useful for you in the third quarter? What are you learning from the way the voices and specialties are woven together?

WRITE ON! Reflect on the categories of prompts that have been most useful for you this quarter.

_____

_____

_____

_____

_____

_____

_____

_____

_____

_____

_____

_____

_____

_____

_____

_____

_____

_____

_____

_____

DATE _____

REVIEW ❖ THE PILLARS OF WELL-BEING. How have the four pillars of well-being (awareness, connection, insight, and purpose) shown up in your life this quarter?

WRITE ON! What is shifting for you in any of the areas of awareness, connection, insight, and purpose? Are you noticing changes in your thinking or process? Write and reflect.

REVIEW ❖ What are you noticing about shifts and changes as you review this quarter? What is different and better?

WRITE ON! What has started to shift in your thinking, feeling, and doing that has made things different and better than they were at the start of this quarter? What have you let go of? What have you invited in? Reflect on the behavioral, mental, emotional, or wellness changes you have noticed over the last thirteen weeks.

_____

_____

_____

_____

_____

_____

_____

_____

_____

_____

_____

_____

_____

_____

_____

_____

_____

_____

_____

REVIEW ❖ WEEKLY REVIEWS. How well have the weekly reviews this quarter helped you observe and track your burnout, writing, intention, and outcomes?

WRITE ON! Write about any observations or correlations you have made in the last thirteen weeks. Compare your notes to those from Week 26. Reflect on any insights or surprises.

_____

_____

_____

_____

_____

QUARTERLY REVIEW ❖ How is the progress of your burnout recovery across the third quarter of the year? Looking back on the last three months, how would you summarize your progress? Where are you now in your burnout recovery program?

On a scale of 1 (low) to 7 (high), rate the third quarter:

Burnout?	①	②	③	④	⑤	⑥	⑦
Writing process?	①	②	③	④	⑤	⑥	⑦
Setting intention?	①	②	③	④	⑤	⑥	⑦
Noticing changes?	①	②	③	④	⑤	⑥	⑦

WRITE ON! Evaluate the past thirteen weeks. What have been your major takeaways? Where do you feel that you're struggling or vulnerable? What have you not yet been able to put into practice? Assess your progress, remembering to be gentle with yourself.

_____

_____

_____

_____

DATE _____

INTENTIONS ❖ You've completed your quarterly check-in, and we're starting a fresh thirteen-week quarter. Let's start by updating your intentions!

WRITE ON! Today, write some intentions for the next quarter. Make these intentions attainable. Finish by writing two or three intentions for this week.

_____

_____

_____

_____

_____

DATE _____

JOURNAL ❖ **WHY WRITING WORKS: SELF-EMPOWERMENT.** Writing encourages self-reliance and self-responsibility. Seeing your life mapped out, one page at a time, makes change observable. It documents how you are empowering yourself to think better-feeling thoughts. At this point in your burnout recovery, you are likely strengthening and seeing evidence of this self-reliance.

WRITE ON! What is different and better in your self-empowerment or self-responsibility? How are you embodying the pillars of well-being (awareness, connection, insight, purpose) in your daily life? Write and reflect.

_____

_____

_____

_____

_____

_____

_____

TRANSITIONS ❖ SAME NAME? On Week 5, Day 3, you named the work transition you wanted. Many months later, it's likely that your original name may not accurately describe your work transition as it is now being lived.

WRITE ON! Review that name and see if it still fits. If it doesn't, choose a different name and describe how it better represents this transition. You might also want to compare and contrast the names, noting the progress represented by the new name. If the original name still fits, write about what it means now.

_____

_____

_____

_____

_____

_____

_____

_____

_____

_____

_____

_____

_____

_____

_____

_____

_____

_____

NEUROPLASTICITY ❖ YOUR BRAIN ON METAPHORS. According to neuroendocrine researcher Robert Sapolsky, the ability to create symbols, metaphors, and figures of speech is all part of what makes us distinctly human. Turning your burnout recovery into a metaphor or symbol is something we've done using several lenses.

WRITE ON! Write a sketch for a character called Burnout Recovery. How does Burnout Recovery appear to you? What are they wearing? What's on their playlist? What's in their refrigerator? What message does Burnout Recovery have for you today? Read back and reflect, noting any surprises or shifts from prior character sketches on burnout.

_____

_____

_____

_____

_____

_____

_____

_____

_____

_____

_____

_____

_____

_____

_____

_____

_____

_____

_____

SIMPLICITY ❖ A RITUAL OF RELEASE. You've been practicing letting go of beliefs, expectations, and habits that led to feelings of burnout. Letting go of a symbolic object can be a way to ritualize that release and free up fresh energy.

WRITE ON! List some possessions and papers that you associate with old burnout-inducing beliefs and patterns. Circle one and write about how you could make a ritual of releasing it. What feelings or insights are generated in letting go of this item?

_____

_____

_____

_____

_____

_____

_____

_____

_____

_____

_____

_____

_____

_____

_____

_____

_____

_____

_____

ANIMAL WISDOM ❖ BACK OFF! No one messes with Badger! These feisty creatures hold their ground and attack to their territories' perimeters when threatened. The absence of boundaries as clear as Badger's can trip you up as you come closer to burnout recovery. Sometimes you need to assertively protect your space, time, and other resources.

WRITE ON! Explore your boundaries. Are they too loose, compromising your resources for your self-care? Are they too rigid, causing you to miss out on opportunities? What's your idea of balance between flexible and firm? How have your boundaries shifted during burnout recovery?

_____

_____

_____

_____

WEEKLY REVIEW ❖ Read back the week's entries, reflections, or both. How do you rank your burnout this week? How do you rank your use of these writing processes? How is the progress of your intentions? Are you noticing changes?

On a scale of 1 (low) to 7 (high), rate your week:

Burnout?	① ② ③ ④ ⑤ ⑥ ⑦
Writing process?	① ② ③ ④ ⑤ ⑥ ⑦
Intentions?	① ② ③ ④ ⑤ ⑥ ⑦
Noticing changes?	① ② ③ ④ ⑤ ⑥ ⑦

WRITE ON! Write observations as you rate your week. Note any connections you may see. Look back over the last four weeks and compare your ratings. Are you noticing progress?

_____

_____

_____

_____

INTENTIONS ❖ You make your intentions stickier when you frame them in positive language. Specify what you want rather than what you want to avoid. It can be surprisingly hard to avoid writing in the negative, so if you slip up, don't worry: just notice it and move on.

WRITE ON! What are three intentions for this week?

_____

_____

_____

_____

_____

_____

ANIMAL WISDOM ❖ CELEBRATE YOUR PERSISTENCE! Camels historically carried treasure over huge desert expanses. They have become symbols of the endurance required for a long journey and the hope of the successful outcome of a pilgrimage. Bring Camel's fortitude with you as you celebrate your patience and stamina that have brought you to this place.

WRITE ON! The treasures that travel with you through the long deserts of burnout include the traits that help you persist. Make a list of personal qualities, core values, strengths, and talents you have called on to support your endurance, then write yourself a thank-you note.

_____

_____

_____

_____

_____

_____

TRANSITIONS ❖ WHAT DO YOU DO? This question is not always easy to answer, especially if you are between jobs or do unpaid work as a homemaker, caretaker, volunteer, or hobbyist. So, forget about these job titles and create a new one! The work you love may combine careers or contain fun descriptors. For example, consider titles like teacher/writer, hobbyist/businessperson, family manager/financial wizard, or semi-retired auto mechanic.

WRITE ON! Create your own work title. Then write the job description. How do you feel when you define your own answer to the question of what you do?

_____

_____

_____

_____

_____

_____

_____

_____

_____

_____

_____

_____

_____

_____

_____

_____

_____

_____

_____

NEUROPLASTICITY ❖ A METAPHOR FOR WELL-BEING. Your brain processes the literal and metaphorical in the same regions, allowing it to treat metaphor as if it were real. Because you have created several metaphors for burnout, your brain has already "fired and wired" this neural circuitry. You can thus more easily install a new metaphor.

WRITE ON! Create a new metaphor to accompany you in this last quarter of your recovery. Rather than explore burnout, let's shift to well-being. What image or symbol represents the well-being you have gained so far and the hope you have for the future? Reflect.

_____

_____

_____

_____

_____

_____

_____

_____

_____

_____

_____

_____

_____

_____

_____

_____

SIMPLICITY ❖ CLUTTER CHECK-IN. You have been working on releasing and reframing different types of clutter for nine months now. Today, let's check in with your progress.

WRITE ON! Think back to the start of this program and the various types of clutter you have worked with, including physical, emotional, mental, and time-related clutter. How has your work with clutter affected your mood or workplace performance? What new habits are you acquiring? What areas would you like to develop further?

_____

_____

_____

_____

_____

_____

_____

_____

_____

_____

_____

_____

_____

_____

_____

_____

_____

_____

WELLNESS ❖ EAT YOUR OMEGA-3S. According to the American Psychological Association, DHA omega-3 essential fatty acids found in algae and fatty fish can help us avoid sensory overload (a common burnout symptom), improve attention, and create calm. If you don't eat fish, many nuts and seeds also contain omega-3s.

WRITE ON! Do a quick search on sources of omega-3 fatty acids and see if you can expand your list to five ways to add this nutrient to your diet. Make notes of recipes or meals that include these essentials.

_____

_____

_____

_____

_____

WEEKLY REVIEW ❖ Read back the week's entries, reflections, or both. How do you rank your burnout this week? How do you rank your use of these writing processes? How is the progress of your intentions? Are you noticing changes?

On a scale of 1 (low) to 7 (high), rate your week:

Burnout?	①	②	③	④	⑤	⑥	⑦
Writing process?	①	②	③	④	⑤	⑥	⑦
Intentions?	①	②	③	④	⑤	⑥	⑦
Noticing changes?	①	②	③	④	⑤	⑥	⑦

WRITE ON! Write observations as you rate your week. Note any connections you may see.

_____

_____

_____

_____

_____

INTENTIONS ❖ What would you like to create this week? Keep your language positive. It's progress, not perfection, that matters!

WRITE ON! What are three intentions for this week? Keep them week-sized.

_____

_____

_____

_____

_____

_____

_____

_____

JOURNAL ❖ **WHY WRITING WORKS: A WITNESS TO HEALING.** Your journal provides a live record of your healing journey. Months and years down the road, you can look back and recognize just how far you've come.

WRITE ON! Today, write with mindfulness about witnessing your own healing process. Who is the healthier self you are becoming?

_____

_____

_____

_____

_____

_____

_____

_____

TRANSITIONS ❖ YOUR DRIVING QUESTION. As you complete this work transition, you will be gathering more resources to create the "new normal." This is a good time to assess your well-being pillar of purpose.

WRITE ON! What is the driving question that moves you forward? It might be "How do I prevent future burnout?," "How do I juice up the skills I haven't used in a while?," or "Do I want to stay in this work long-term?" Note ideas on how you can find the answer. Are there people or resources that could help?

_____

_____

_____

_____

_____

_____

_____

_____

_____

_____

_____

_____

_____

_____

_____

_____

_____

_____

NEUROPLASTICITY ❖ MAKING METAPHOR TANGIBLE. Your efficient brain can link your words to your sense of touch. Find an object that serves as a metaphor for your changing self-care—perhaps a feather to feel lighter or a stone to symbolize the heft and significance of a new practice. Incorporate this object into your daily routine by placing it in view of your desk or primary workstation.

WRITE ON! Hold or have in view a physical object to represent your self-care metaphor. Write about how this object represents the qualities of self-care. Savor the feeling this metaphor brings. Reflect.

_____

_____

_____

_____

_____

_____

_____

_____

_____

_____

_____

_____

_____

_____

_____

_____

_____

_____

SIMPLICITY ❖ PACKING LIGHT. When traveling through life, it is tempting to overpack. In the past you may have overburdened yourself by trying to have, do, and be everything. The clearer you are about who you are and what's important to you, the more likely it is that you can pack light.

WRITE ON! Make a packing list for your life going forward. What is important to bring? What can you leave behind? Read and reflect on what insights emerged.

_____

_____

_____

_____

_____

_____

_____

_____

_____

_____

_____

_____

_____

_____

_____

_____

_____

_____

_____

_____

_____

_____

ANIMAL WISDOM ❖ CONNECT WITH YOUR PAST. Salmon swim upriver from the ocean to their birthplaces to mate. They'll endure many hardships to make this significant and life-sustaining journey. Generation after generation, Salmon undergo this ancestral ritual.

WRITE ON! Although it might not have been burnout, we each have ancestors who endured hardship. What did they endure, and how did they manage hard times? Write down one of their stories. How can you apply their lessons to your current recovery?

_____

_____

_____

_____

WEEKLY REVIEW ❖ Read back the week's entries, reflections, or both. How do you rank your burnout this week? How do you rank your use of these writing processes? How is the progress of your intentions? Are you noticing changes?

On a scale of 1 (low) to 7 (high), rate your week:

Burnout?	① ② ③ ④ ⑤ ⑥ ⑦
Writing process?	① ② ③ ④ ⑤ ⑥ ⑦
Intentions?	① ② ③ ④ ⑤ ⑥ ⑦
Noticing changes?	① ② ③ ④ ⑤ ⑥ ⑦

WRITE ON! Write observations as you rate your week. Note any connections you may see. Look back over the last four weeks and compare your ratings. Are you noticing progress?

_____

_____

_____

_____

INTENTIONS ❖ As you have worked with the pillars of well-being, you may find that your intentions reflect the values of awareness, connection, insight, and purpose. Setting intentions themed around these pillars can amplify outcomes.

WRITE ON! As you write your intentions this week, keep the pillars of well-being in the foreground. Can you craft intentions that reflect an orientation to well-being?

_____

_____

_____

_____

_____

JOURNAL ❖ WHY WRITING WORKS: CLOSURE WITH THE PAST. Holding on to a past that cannot change produces anxiety and drains energy. Keeping old resentment, guilt, shame, blame, anger, and hurt alive can leave you feeling stuck, ill-tempered, and uncertain about your own value. Your journal offers a safe place to vent, process, and release stored feelings about past events. This closure offers opportunities for forgiveness of yourself and others.

WRITE ON! Now that you are moving into a new way of burnout recovery, what in your life are you ready to move on from? What are you ready to release?

_____

_____

_____

_____

_____

_____

TRANSITIONS ❖ WRONG TURN? No plan is perfect. Setbacks happen, but we can learn from them. There may be missed opportunities or wrong turns. With each of these, note what you learned and what will help you avoid some of these in the future.

WRITE ON! Think about a work misstep or missed opportunity that has occurred and what you learned from it. How are you getting back in the driver's seat?

_____

_____

_____

_____

_____

_____

_____

_____

_____

_____

_____

_____

_____

_____

_____

_____

_____

_____

_____

_____

NEUROPLASTICITY ✦ SOMETHING BIGGER. Remember that research tells us well-being is a skill that can be learned. Feeling a connection to something bigger than yourself helps you strengthen this skill.

WRITE ON! Make a list of the things that are bigger than yourself and with which you are deeply connected. Get as vast and expansive as you like. Describe how your connections give you strength.

_____

_____

_____

_____

_____

_____

_____

_____

_____

_____

_____

_____

_____

_____

_____

_____

_____

_____

_____

_____

_____

_____

WELLNESS ❖ DEFEATING GIANTS. In his book *David and Goliath*, journalist Malcolm Gladwell notes that courage is not predetermined but acquired by making it through tough times with reflective awareness. He calls these moments "near misses" and reminds us that they are the building blocks for resilience.

WRITE ON! Name a time this past year when you feared you wouldn't make it through an internal, external, or perceived difficulty. List some factors (such as people, personal strengths, or outside circumstances) that helped you weather the storm. Savor the present awareness by writing a gratitude statement about your courage.

_____

_____

_____

_____

_____

_____

_____

_____

_____

_____

_____

_____

_____

_____

_____

_____

_____

_____

_____

SIMPLICITY ❖ MAKING SPACE. As you've traveled through this book, you've been actively shaping your perspective and affecting your reality. As you've been clearing the clutter from your home, head, heart, and schedule, you might be making space for dreams, visions, and goals that you have delayed or decided were not possible for you.

WRITE ON! What are you making space for? Make a list or draw the things that come to mind. Reflect on your responses.

_____

_____

_____

_____

_____

_____

WEEKLY REVIEW ❖ Read back the week's entries, reflections, or both. How do you rank your burnout this week? How do you rank your use of these writing processes? How is the progress of your intentions? Are you noticing changes?

On a scale of 1 (low) to 7 (high), rate your week:

Burnout?	① ② ③ ④ ⑤ ⑥ ⑦
Writing process?	① ② ③ ④ ⑤ ⑥ ⑦
Intentions?	① ② ③ ④ ⑤ ⑥ ⑦
Noticing changes?	① ② ③ ④ ⑤ ⑥ ⑦

WRITE ON! Write observations as you rate your week. Note any connections you may see.

_____

_____

_____

_____

INTENTIONS ❖ What would you like to create this week? Remember to use positive language.

WRITE ON! What are three intentions for this week?

_____

_____

_____

_____

_____

_____

_____

_____

WELLNESS ❖ **GROW THE GOOD.** Our minds create stories all the time, and as you now know, they are naturally more attracted to the negative than the positive. One way we can use our mindfulness skills is to practice "growing the good" by consciously reflecting on positive thoughts and past successes.

WRITE ON! Read through some of your past entries. Make a list of favorites. Give each entry a story title descriptive enough for you to recall a few details when you read it. Choose one entry to write about in detail. Note why this entry is precious to you.

_____

_____

_____

_____

_____

_____

TRANSITIONS ❖ IMAGINE THIS. In Week 35, Day 2, you learned how to jump time using altered perspective. A "future story" gives you the chance to imagine what you'll look back on. Imagine it is this time, next year. Notice what has changed for the better in your work.

WRITE ON! Date your entry one year from today's date. Write your future story. If it's helpful, start with something like, "I look back on the past year and feel good about how I have transitioned from work burnout. I have. . . ."

_____

_____

_____

_____

_____

_____

_____

_____

_____

_____

_____

_____

_____

_____

_____

_____

_____

_____

_____

NEUROPLASTICITY ❖ PURPOSE AND CORE VALUES. We often imagine that our happiness is linked to finding our single overarching life purpose. However, according to Dahl, Wilson-Mendenhall, and Davidson, purpose is fulfilled through the core values and ethics that guide our daily life.

WRITE ON! Create a cluster (see Week 8, Day 2) with the phrase "My Core Values" in the center. When you've completed the cluster, step back, review what you drew, and write about what you see. Reflect on how these core values sustain your well-being.

_____

_____

_____

_____

_____

_____

_____

_____

_____

_____

_____

_____

_____

_____

_____

_____

_____

_____

_____

SIMPLICITY ❖ A CALM CENTER. You have likely made significant progress in decluttering and simplifying your workspace. Yet it may still tend toward chaos in some areas. It can be helpful to intentionally clear an area that attracts disarray and then place something there that represents calm, grounded energy.

WRITE ON! What chaotic area could use a makeover? Write about that space, how you could clear it, and what you could place there to conjure calm.

_____

_____

_____

_____

_____

_____

_____

_____

_____

_____

_____

_____

_____

_____

_____

_____

_____

_____

_____

DATE _____ WEEK **44** • DAY **6**

ANIMAL WISDOM ❖ REMEMBER WHEN. Famous for her long and clear memory, Elephant never forgets. Even after years of separation, Elephant recognizes old friends, animal and human alike. Now that your mind is clearer and less focused on the exhaustion, disappointment, and despair of burnout, bring back from memory the people, places, and things that sustain you.

WRITE ON! Write a list of magical moments from pre-burnout times. Gather large milestones, celebrations, and anniversaries as well as smaller moments, such as a good meal, a charming gift, or satisfying encounter with a friend. How can you re-engage?

_____

_____

_____

_____

DATE _____ WEEK **44** • DAY **7**

WEEKLY REVIEW ❖ Read back the week's entries, reflections, or both. How do you rank your burnout this week? How do you rank your use of these writing processes? How is the progress of your intentions? Are you noticing changes?

On a scale of 1 (low) to 7 (high), rate your week:

Burnout? ① ② ③ ④ ⑤ ⑥ ⑦

Writing process? ① ② ③ ④ ⑤ ⑥ ⑦

Intentions? ① ② ③ ④ ⑤ ⑥ ⑦

Noticing changes? ① ② ③ ④ ⑤ ⑥ ⑦

WRITE ON! Write observations as you rate your week. Note any connections you may see. Look back over the last four weeks and compare your ratings. Are you noticing progress?

_____

_____

_____

_____

INTENTIONS ❖ Your current reality is no doubt changing, and you may find that that current reality is matching or nearly matching your vision. That's when you know you are ready for a new vision, which may be the next step that takes you closer to actualization.

WRITE ON! Today, write about any larger visions that have manifested because of your intentions. If it's time to update a vision, do so. Then write three intentions for this week.

_____

_____

_____

_____

_____

JOURNAL ❖ WHY WRITING WORKS: YOU. The reason writing works for any individual is because that person has put intention, attention, and action into creating a life and documented it. If you've come this far, you're likely finding benefits such as improved mood, increased clarity, more life balance, or enhanced interpersonal relationships.

WRITE ON! This is the last in the series of "Why Writing Works" prompts. Looking back, why has writing worked for you during this program? What are you discovering? Write about the benefits you are gaining from this journal.

_____

_____

_____

_____

_____

_____

_____

TRANSITIONS ❖ PAPER TRAIL. Writing keeps a record of your transition—what is happening, what needs work, and what steps to take next. The power of writing helps ensure that your burnout does not return—or, if it does, that you have the awareness to proactively respond.

WRITE ON! Create a prompt that you will use for a regular check-in on your work renewal and practice responding to it. Something simple like "How's it going?" will do. Write briefly about what is going well and what needs more attention. Make notes about building bridges between your current and desired realities.

_____

_____

_____

_____

_____

_____

_____

_____

_____

_____

_____

_____

_____

_____

_____

_____

_____

_____

NEUROPLASTICITY ❖ PURPOSE IN EVERYDAY LIFE. According to Dahl, Wilson-Mendenhall, and Davidson, creating a link between our meaningful core values and our everyday lives helps us experience a sense of purpose. Daily activities can be an expression of values.

WRITE ON! Make a list of mundane tasks, such as a chore or something you do by rote or habit (like unloading the dishwasher, commuting, recycling, or paying bills). Choose one item and write about the values it embodies. For instance, commuting could represent your commitment to your work. Savor this new awareness of the purpose behind this everyday activity.

_____

_____

_____

_____

_____

_____

_____

_____

_____

_____

_____

_____

_____

_____

_____

_____

_____

_____

SIMPLICITY ❖ HOW'S YOUR TIME CLUTTER? The pillars of well-being—awareness, connection, insight, and purpose—carry over to all aspects of your burnout recovery, including your schedule. Which structured practices have you learned to help with time management?

WRITE ON! Today, reflect on the time management–related patterns and habits that you have changed. How have you grown more mindful of time as a resource? How might this awareness impact your future relationship with time?

_____

_____

_____

_____

_____

_____

_____

_____

_____

_____

_____

_____

_____

_____

_____

_____

_____

_____

_____

_____

WELLNESS ❖ SEEING CLEARLY. All day, your eyes sort data or take in a variety of information that needs your attention —emails, video calls, documents, spreadsheets. Mindful seeing, without thought or judgment, can be a welcome meditation for the eyes. It also boosts insight.

WRITE ON! Find a scenic window or location. Set a three-minute timer and take in the view. Notice subtle movements such as clouds shifting or tree branches rustling. Imagine that you have never seen this view before. Write about your experience. Reflect on how you will apply this new "vision" to your life.

_____

_____

_____

_____

WEEKLY REVIEW ❖ Read back the week's entries, reflections, or both. How do you rank your burnout this week? How do you rank your use of these writing processes? How is the progress of your intentions? Are you noticing changes?

On a scale of 1 (low) to 7 (high), rate your week:

Burnout?	① ② ③ ④ ⑤ ⑥ ⑦
Writing process?	① ② ③ ④ ⑤ ⑥ ⑦
Intentions?	① ② ③ ④ ⑤ ⑥ ⑦
Noticing changes?	① ② ③ ④ ⑤ ⑥ ⑦

WRITE ON! Write observations as you rate your week. Note any connections you may see.

_____

_____

_____

_____

_____

DATE _____   WEEK **46** • D_{AY} **1**

INTENTIONS ❖ This would be a good week to review the last month or six weeks of intentions to see if there are those that have fallen dormant but are still viable.

WRITE ON! Are there carry-over intentions from your "intention audit"? If so, choose one and write a week-sized intention that will move it from background to foreground. Then write two others that are current for this week.

_____

_____

_____

_____

_____

_____

DATE _____   WEEK **46** • D_{AY} **2**

JOURNAL ❖ **IF YOU FALTER.** Although it's nice to have freedom again after intensive focus, it can also leave us feeling a little wobbly. If you start to slip back into old burnout thoughts, feelings, or behaviors, have a rescue kit handy.

WRITE ON! Describe your rescue kit. What are five specific tools, techniques, or strategies that you will enact immediately if you falter?

_____

_____

_____

_____

_____

_____

_____

_____

_____

TRANSITIONS ❖ TOUCHSTONES OF WELL-BEING. One dictionary definition of touchstone is "a standard or criterion by which something is judged or recognized." Your well-being touchstones are the qualities that keep you in balance when your energy or stamina flags.

WRITE ON! Make a list of your well-being touchstones. These might include qualities such as energized, creative, connected, hopeful, or productive. They could include your core values. Next, list any unresolved burnout symptoms. Pair your touchstones with different symptoms. If you recalled a specific quality or value the next time you had a particular symptom, what might happen? Reflect on surprises or insights.

DATE _____

WEEK 46 • DAY 4

NEUROPLASTICITY ❖ FINDING PURPOSE IN CHALLENGES. Often, challenges, internal conflicts, or setbacks in your burnout recovery are connected to core values that you can't fully express. For instance, you may strongly value freedom, but you work in a rigid and inflexible environment. One way to address these challenges is to invoke a different core value—say, patience—to help resolve the blockage.

WRITE ON! Write about a time, perhaps during a phase of active burnout, when you were prevented from expressing a core value. What other core value might have helped you through the situation? How? Reflect.

_____

_____

_____

_____

_____

_____

_____

_____

_____

_____

_____

_____

_____

_____

_____

_____

_____

_____

_____

SIMPLICITY ❖ SIMPLIFICATION STRATEGIES. We live multifaceted lives in a complex world, yet you can bring the intention to streamline, curate, and put your focus and resources where they matter most.

WRITE ON! Review the ways that you have simplified your life, schedule, routine, and work in your burnout recovery. Just as importantly, *how* have you achieved this? Have you used discipline? Focus? Curation? Streamlining? Donating? Shredding? What are the simplification strategies that have worked best for you? Reflect on how you can integrate these simplification strategies going forward.

_____

_____

_____

_____

_____

_____

_____

_____

_____

_____

_____

_____

_____

_____

_____

_____

_____

_____

_____

ANIMAL WISDOM ❖ RESPOND ANOTHER WAY. Oyster creates a beautiful pearl to protect herself from irritation. Instead of giving in to discomfort, she wraps a lustrous coating around the little things that get inside and bother her. Remember Oyster the next time you are annoyed.

WRITE ON! Make a list of the little irritations in your life and write reality-based better-feeling thoughts to nullify their annoyance. Put the list within your sight so you can return to them whenever you feel an irksome prickle.

_____

_____

_____

_____

WEEKLY REVIEW ❖ Read back the week's entries, reflections, or both. How do you rank your burnout this week? How do you rank your use of these writing processes? How is the progress of your intentions? Are you noticing changes?

On a scale of 1 (low) to 7 (high), rate your week:

Burnout?	① ② ③ ④ ⑤ ⑥ ⑦
Writing process?	① ② ③ ④ ⑤ ⑥ ⑦
Intentions?	① ② ③ ④ ⑤ ⑥ ⑦
Noticing changes?	① ② ③ ④ ⑤ ⑥ ⑦

WRITE ON! Write observations as you rate your week. Note any connections you may see.

_____

_____

_____

_____

_____

DATE _____ **Week 47 • Day 1**

INTENTIONS ❖ What do you want to do, be, or have at the end of this week?

WRITE ON! Write three intentions that are focused on a task you want to accomplish, the state of mind that you want to be in as you complete the week, and at least one thing you want to shift this week.

_____
_____
_____
_____
_____
_____

DATE _____ **Week 47 • Day 2**

SIMPLICITY ❖ LEARNING TO WORK WITH TIME. In the past, you may have struggled with time. Now you've practiced engaging with time in some new ways. You are learning to work with time in a way that is more productive and purposeful.

WRITE ON! Write a poem beginning with these two lines:

Time and I are learning
how to work together.

Don't worry about whether you're a poet. Give the poem a title. Read and reflect on what emerged.

_____
_____
_____
_____
_____
_____

TRANSITIONS ❖ A PEAK MOMENT. A peak moment is one that synthesizes and integrates all the best aspects of yourself or your environment into one sensory experience. It can serve as a light and support in the new way.

WRITE ON! Bring to mind one moment of work that feels good, one when you liked what you were doing, who you were with, and the outcome. Describe this experience in detail, using verbs, adjectives, and words that create a picture showing that you have banished burnout. Reflect on what came up.

_____

_____

_____

_____

_____

_____

_____

_____

_____

_____

_____

_____

_____

_____

_____

_____

_____

_____

_____

_____

NEUROPLASTICITY ❖ THE EXAMINED LIFE. Socrates, known as the father of Western philosophy, is credited with saying that the unexamined life isn't worth living. Self-inquiry involves knowing your assumptions, particularly the rigid beliefs that contribute to suffering and burnout, and challenging them. All this examination has helped you gain insight, a pillar of well-being.

WRITE ON! Make a list of 3–5 rigid assumptions or beliefs you had when burnout was at its worst. Describe how they have transformed. Note the fresh realizations.

_____

_____

_____

_____

_____

_____

_____

_____

_____

_____

_____

_____

_____

_____

_____

_____

_____

_____

ANIMAL WISDOM ❖ TAKE YOURSELF LIGHTLY. At the Duke Lemur Center, lemurs of several species live in a huge habitat. These natives of Madagascar delight in swinging across a forest canopy with playful grace. As you turn toward the completion of your burnout recovery program, it is important to bring back the art of play and delight.

WRITE ON! See if you can find humor in the tedium of your daily routine. Write about an annoying or disruptive incident as if you were sharing it on stage as a standup comic. Reflect.

_____

_____

_____

_____

_____

_____

_____

_____

_____

_____

_____

_____

_____

_____

_____

_____

_____

_____

_____

WELLNESS ❖ MISSION ACCOMPLISHED. According to the National Institutes of Health, the degree to which people feel empowered carries a positive impact on their ability to maintain and adopt a healthy lifestyle. Most successful companies have a guiding statement that governs their purpose and outlines their goals. Be your own wellness CEO!

WRITE ON! Identify some of the new wellness practices or routines you have practiced this year. Writing in the present tense, craft a personal-wellness vision statement that describes your commitments to your overall health. Post the statement in a place where you can read it easily and daily.

_____

_____

_____

_____

_____

WEEKLY REVIEW ❖ Read back the week's entries, reflections, or both. How do you rank your burnout this week? How do you rank your use of these writing processes? How is the progress of your intentions? Are you noticing changes?

On a scale of 1 (low) to 7 (high), rate your week:

Burnout?	① ② ③ ④ ⑤ ⑥ ⑦
Writing process?	① ② ③ ④ ⑤ ⑥ ⑦
Intentions?	① ② ③ ④ ⑤ ⑥ ⑦
Noticing changes?	① ② ③ ④ ⑤ ⑥ ⑦

WRITE ON! Write observations as you rate your week. Note any connections you may see.

_____

_____

_____

_____

INTENTIONS ❖ The habit of intention-setting can be done on a daily as well as a weekly basis. It begins with the usual setting of three weekly intentions, then continues with daily intentions to advance one or more weekly intentions in a specific way. Perhaps you have found yourself organically following this path.

WRITE ON! Write your usual three intentions for this week. Each day, try writing two or three sub-intentions to support the weekly intentions. These can be very small steps that accrue quickly.

_____

_____

_____

_____

_____

ANIMAL WISDOM ❖ HELP CLEAN UP THE MESS. Consider how Vulture supports the needs of his community with his capacity to clear away the debris of the dead, which would be toxic to the living if left as is. Many parts of our workplaces, families, and communities need support and assistance, whether they be food banks or community programs for at-risk youth.

WRITE ON! As you experience a restored sense of well-being, how might you reach out to help someone or something that is still struggling? How might you help improve the well-being of a family, group, or project you care about?

_____

_____

_____

_____

_____

_____

_____

TRANSITIONS ❖ IS THERE MORE? You have made great strides with transitioning from work burnout. What else do you want to change about your work or career growth? Maybe, more than you first thought, you wish to change your job or the type of work. Is there another shift that you want to grow toward? Your workplace transition is an ongoing, fluid process rather than a static end-point.

WRITE ON! Write about any changes in your work that you want to make next. You don't need to do anything else except ponder what that might be. You are just thinking out loud on the page.

_____

_____

_____

_____

_____

_____

_____

_____

_____

_____

_____

_____

_____

_____

_____

_____

_____

_____

_____

NEUROPLASTICITY ❖ ONE LOVING ACTION. Our love and compassion for others and ourselves provide reliable support during difficult times. It may be tempting to shame yourself when you are less than your best, but your brain learns more and builds well-being habits more quickly when you motivate yourself with compassion and love.

WRITE ON! Write about one loving action, whether it is directed toward yourself or others, that you can take today in service of your well-being. Then take that action and write about the outcome. Reflect.

_____

_____

_____

_____

_____

_____

_____

_____

_____

_____

_____

_____

_____

_____

_____

_____

_____

_____

_____

WELLNESS ❖ BRAVE CONVERSATIONS. Mindfulness teacher Jon Kabat-Zinn reminds us that "no one can listen to your body for you. . . . To grow and heal, you have to take responsibility for listening to it yourself." The journal dialogue (see Week 30, Day 2) teaches how to listen carefully to your body and heed the offered wisdom

WRITE ON! Select an aspect of your health or personality, perhaps energy level, patience, or fear. Create a dialogue with a personification of this aspect. Remember to thank your dialogue partner. Make sure you have the last word. Read and reflect.

_____

_____

_____

_____

_____

_____

_____

_____

_____

_____

_____

_____

_____

_____

_____

_____

_____

_____

SIMPLICITY ❖ LIGHTENING UP. Life can get so heavy. But you've been lightening the load as you've gently and purposefully removed clutter from your home, head, heart, and schedule.

WRITE ON! How does this "lightening up" process feel to you? You can use a metaphor to describe your feelings or begin with this springboard: "As I am feeling lighter, I notice more _____."

_____

_____

_____

_____

_____

WEEKLY REVIEW ❖ Read back the week's entries, reflections, or both. How do you rank your burnout this week? How do you rank your use of these writing processes? How is the progress of your intentions? Are you noticing changes?

On a scale of 1 (low) to 7 (high), rate your week:

Burnout?	①	②	③	④	⑤	⑥	⑦
Writing process?	①	②	③	④	⑤	⑥	⑦
Intentions?	①	②	③	④	⑤	⑥	⑦
Noticing changes?	①	②	③	④	⑤	⑥	⑦

WRITE ON! Write observations as you rate your week. Note any connections you may see. Look back over the last four weeks and compare your ratings. Are you noticing progress?

_____

_____

_____

_____

DATE _____   WEEK 49 • DAY 1

INTENTIONS ❖ Taking your intentions to heart each week could be paying off by now as you move closer and closer to recovery.

WRITE ON! What are three intentions for this week? These can be related to any area of your life. Break larger intentions into week-sized bites.

_____

_____

_____

_____

_____

_____

_____

DATE _____   WEEK 49 • DAY 2

JOURNAL ❖ **JOURNAL CONTINUATION.** How will you continue to journal after this year? It's not necessary to write every day. Two to four times a week will be enough to set weekly intentions, process thoughts and reflections, note progress, and deepen specific habits. You can also keep a notebook in your bag and write five-minute sprints on the go. If you miss some days, forgive yourself and move on.

WRITE ON! What feels like the best journal plan going forward? Listen to your heart and intuition. List the guidance that comes forward.

_____

_____

_____

_____

_____

_____

_____

TRANSITIONS ❖ LEFTOVERS. As you review the parts of your work transitions, you might come across some unfinished business that you would like to take care of. Perhaps you want to let go of another item, revisit an interesting idea from the in-between phase of your transition, or thank someone else who helped you. Look through your journal for any leftovers.

WRITE ON! If you find an important piece of unfinished business, do you want to take care of it? What would it take? Write and reflect.

_____

_____

_____

_____

_____

_____

_____

_____

_____

_____

_____

_____

_____

_____

_____

_____

_____

_____

_____

_____

_____

NEUROPLASTICITY ❖ INSPIRATION, INTENTION, ACTION. Inspiration helps you take the first step toward meaningful change, but it doesn't last long. According to Dahl, we also need intention to serve as a bridge from inspiration to action, particularly when the action taken is in the form of small, simple steps.

WRITE ON! Remembering that the brain loves metaphor, write about a memorable walk or hike you have taken. Place your written attention on the experience of arriving at your destination, all by putting one foot in front of the other. Reflect on the power of one step at a time to meet a goal.

_____
_____
_____
_____
_____
_____
_____
_____
_____
_____
_____
_____
_____
_____
_____
_____
_____
_____
_____
_____
_____

ANIMAL WISDOM ❖ ALWAYS BE AT HOME. Land Tortoise can live up to 150 years within his domed shell. During burnout recovery, perhaps you have learned to feel more at home in your own body, mind, heart, and spirit.

WRITE ON! Write about what your inner home feels like now, and how you can nurture it to maximize your well-being.

_____

_____

_____

_____

_____

_____

_____

_____

_____

_____

_____

_____

_____

_____

_____

_____

_____

_____

_____

_____

_____

_____

WELLNESS ❖ CELEBRATE GOOD TIMES! So often when we are driven by a goal, we forget to focus on our wins, simply moving on to the next task on the to-do list. Positive psychology researcher Teresa Amabile notes that frequently tracking small wins increases motivation.

WRITE ON! List a few of your recent small achievements. Write yourself a letter that appreciates these accomplishments. What ritual can you create to reward yourself? Read your letter aloud, listening deeply and breathing in as you recognize all your hard work.

_____

_____

_____

_____

WEEKLY REVIEW ❖ Read back the week's entries, reflections, or both. How do you rank your burnout this week? How do you rank your use of these writing processes? How is the progress of your intentions? Are you noticing changes?

On a scale of 1 (low) to 7 (high), rate your week:

Burnout?	①	②	③	④	⑤	⑥	⑦
Writing process?	①	②	③	④	⑤	⑥	⑦
Intentions?	①	②	③	④	⑤	⑥	⑦
Noticing changes?	①	②	③	④	⑤	⑥	⑦

WRITE ON! Write observations as you rate your week. Note any connections you may see.

_____

_____

_____

_____

_____

INTENTIONS ❖ The habit of intention-setting is one that will support you for years to come. Continue setting weekly intentions for yourself well after your burnout recovery!

WRITE ON! Set three intentions for this week, framed in positive language.

_____

_____

_____

_____

_____

_____

JOURNAL ❖ A GOODBYE LETTER. We are coming to the end of this yearlong journey. You've covered a lot of ground and written thousands of words. You're a lot different than when you started! Think back to who you were then, and who you are now.

WRITE ON! Write a goodbye letter to the unhappy, stressed parts of "you" that started this program. You have been there for yourself through this whole book. Give a written standing ovation to that brave you who got here after a full year of consistent effort.

_____

_____

_____

_____

_____

_____

TRANSITIONS ❖ PREPARING FOR THE FUTURE. How we work changes throughout our lives. These days we may have many jobs, paid or unpaid, and perform several types of work. We are always going to have work transitions. If something suddenly changes in your work and you need to make another big transition, what steps will you take to prepare, based on what you now know?

WRITE ON! Write the first steps you plan to take if you face a future work transition. Build in some steps for burnout prevention. You can make a list or write a short paragraph.

_____

_____

_____

_____

_____

_____

_____

_____

_____

_____

_____

_____

_____

_____

_____

_____

_____

_____

NEUROPLASTICITY ❖ YOUR NORTH STAR. Your North Star is the inner guidance that steers you in the direction of your optimum well-being. When you stay attuned to this guidance, you may find that you find deeper meaning and purpose in your daily interactions.

WRITE ON! How has your North Star shifted during this time of healing? Is your inner GPS recalibrated? Write and reflect. Going forward, if you write in the morning, connect your daily activities to your sense of purpose. If you write in the evening, review your day with an eye toward those connections.

_____

_____

_____

_____

_____

_____

_____

_____

_____

_____

_____

_____

_____

_____

_____

_____

_____

_____

SIMPLICITY ❖ A RITUAL OF FORGIVENESS. Look around your workspace to see if there are mementos or objects related to stressful events, mistakes, or projects you'll never get around to. Can you release them and clear space to step fully into your future?

WRITE ON! Gather up items that remind you of past disappointment, frustration, shame, or guilt. Check in to make sure you're ready to release them. Then create a forgiveness ritual. Hold each item in turn and write, "I release this [item name]. I forgive myself and anyone associated with it." Close by giving permission for a fresh start.

_____

_____

_____

_____

_____

_____

_____

_____

_____

_____

_____

_____

_____

_____

_____

_____

_____

_____

_____

DATE _____   WEEK **50** • DAY **6**

ANIMAL WISDOM ❖ NOTHING IS WASTED. Buffalo gives his meat for food, his hide and sinews for garments, and his bones for weapons and adornments. In return, Buffalo's people respect and value every aspect of him. Nothing is wasted.

WRITE ON! Every day this year has moved you one step closer to restoring your well-being from burnout. No moment has been wasted, not the setbacks nor the downturns. Today, write about something that, at the time, seemed like wasted effort, time, or money. Reflect on how that obstacle moved you closer to this moment.

_____

_____

_____

_____

_____

DATE _____   WEEK **50** • DAY **7**

WEEKLY REVIEW ❖ Read back the week's entries, reflections, or both. How do you rank your burnout this week? How do you rank your use of these writing processes? How is the progress of your intentions? Are you noticing changes?

On a scale of 1 (low) to 7 (high), rate your week:

Burnout?	①	②	③	④	⑤	⑥	⑦
Writing process?	①	②	③	④	⑤	⑥	⑦
Intentions?	①	②	③	④	⑤	⑥	⑦
Noticing changes?	①	②	③	④	⑤	⑥	⑦

WRITE ON! Write observations as you rate your week. Note any connections you see.

_____

_____

_____

_____

INTENTIONS ❖ Congratulations! You have made it through nearly a whole year of intention-setting! What are the results you have to show for it?

WRITE ON! What has been the power of intention-setting for you this year? Reflect on your new habit of setting weekly intentions.

_____

_____

_____

_____

_____

_____

ANIMAL WISDOM ❖ **ADOPT A WISE GUIDE.** You have written by keeping in mind the perspective of many animals, whether footed, feathered, furred, or finned. Perhaps some animals captured your imagination in this journey.

WRITE ON! Which animal metaphors have stayed with you? Write and reflect on the significance of one animal's wisdom for you this year.

_____

_____

_____

_____

_____

_____

_____

_____

_____

DATE _____   **WEEK 51 • DAY 3**

TRANSITIONS ❖ FINDING THE NEW NORMAL. Every time, you transition to a new way, you create a new normal. Like moving to a new house, it takes a while for the change to feel natural and comfortable. Be patient as you settle into your new way.

WRITE ON! Think about one change you are making to banish burnout. What will signal that you are comfortable with the change? Start by writing a response to this prompt: "I will know I have transitioned into this change, when I experience _____."

_____

_____

_____

_____

_____

_____

_____

_____

_____

_____

_____

_____

_____

_____

_____

_____

_____

_____

_____

NEUROPLASTICITY ❖ YOUR CHANGING BRAIN. Think back to when you started this program, and who you were then. What has changed?

WRITE ON! Write the phrase MY CHANGING BRAIN or MY BURNOUT RECOVERY vertically down the page, one letter at a time. Now write an alphapoem (see Week 18, Day 2) about the changes you have made this year. Write quickly and don't overthink it. Take what comes. When you're finished, read it aloud to yourself, knowing that you have just stretched into poetry and are flourishing. Put your poem on your refrigerator!

_____

_____

_____

_____

_____

_____

_____

_____

_____

_____

_____

_____

_____

_____

_____

_____

_____

_____

SIMPLICITY ❖ A TITLE FOR THE YEAR. It can be helpful to give a title to the time ahead to help guide your focus and energy. A title can also help you summarize the day, week, month, or year you've just traveled through.

WRITE ON! Write a list of titles you would give to the year you just traveled through and a list of titles that you'd like to give to the year ahead. Circle your favorites.

_____
_____
_____
_____
_____
_____
_____
_____
_____
_____
_____
_____
_____
_____
_____
_____
_____
_____
_____

WELLNESS ❖ STAYING IN THE NEW STORY. Change is hard work. Out of habit, you might lapse into dwelling on the past or indulge fears of losing what you have gained. Chances are, you will need to train your brain to hold onto some of your changes.

WRITE ON! Start by completing this sentence in multiple ways: "I used to _____, but now I _____." Write for ten minutes about some of the changes you have made this past year. Though our stories continue, close this one with a happy ending that focuses on a few of your recent positive changes.

_____

_____

_____

_____

WEEKLY REVIEW ❖ Read back the week's entries, reflections, or both. How do you rank your burnout this week? How do you rank your use of these writing processes? How is the progress of your intentions? Are you noticing changes?

On a scale of 1 (low) to 7 (high), rate your week:

Burnout?	①	②	③	④	⑤	⑥	⑦
Writing process?	①	②	③	④	⑤	⑥	⑦
Intentions?	①	②	③	④	⑤	⑥	⑦
Noticing changes?	①	②	③	④	⑤	⑥	⑦

WRITE ON! Write observations as you rate your week. Note any connections you may see. Look back over the last three weeks and compare your ratings. Are you noticing progress?

_____

_____

_____

_____

DATE _____   WEEK 52 • DAY 1

ONE-YEAR INTENTIONS ❖ You have been setting week-sized intentions in this journal, but you can also gaze at a horizon far in the future, such as a year or five years. Think about what you want for yourself going forward.

WRITE ON! Write 5 to 7 intentions for the next 365 days. What do you want to do, be, and have? If you could make significant progress toward some of these intentions, how would your life be different and better?

_____

_____

_____

_____

_____

_____

DATE _____   WEEK 52 • DAY 2

ANIMAL WISDOM ❖ **ALWAYS BE DISTINCT!** Every Zebra has a distinct pattern. While she may look like her herd mates from afar, she is a unique individual, just as you are. Zebras recognize one another within a large herd. As we come to the end of this year, celebrate the uniqueness that has emerged for you.

WRITE ON! Write yourself a note of appreciation for your distinct individuality. Going forward, however you choose to express yourself, Zebra tells you to take a brave approach. Even your most distinctive acts won't result in exile from humanity.

_____

_____

_____

_____

_____

_____

TRANSITIONS ❖ TRANSITION IN A NUTSHELL. You have experienced a transition into burnout, then into recovery. You have learned new ways of working with these changes. You started by letting go, then navigated the messy middle, and have now crossed the threshold into the new way. You have moved through each stage in your own personal way.

WRITE ON! Write for as long as you wish about the transition process and what you have learned about your personal transition style. Return to this information for a future transition.

_____

_____

_____

_____

_____

_____

_____

_____

_____

_____

_____

_____

_____

_____

_____

_____

_____

_____

_____

_____

NEUROPLASTICITY ❖ A GROWTH MINDSET. Research scientist Christine Wilson-Mendenhall reports it is important to understand not only who we are, but also how we are always changing. This notion serves as the foundation of a growth mindset, which helps you navigate difficult circumstances and affects how you feel about yourself during challenges.

WRITE ON! This year has been one of change. Celebrate your improved well-being by adopting a growth mindset about the future. What skills do you take with you? Write about the new habits you've developed to strengthen the four pillars of well-being.

_____

_____

_____

_____

_____

_____

_____

_____

_____

_____

_____

_____

_____

_____

_____

_____

_____

_____

SIMPLICITY ❖ YOUR WISE SELF. You have been learning, growing, and practicing new patterns of thought and action, shedding clutter, and creating spaciousness. As you come to the end of this book, invite some words of wisdom from yourself.

WRITE ON! What message does your wisest self have for you? What does it want to be sure you'll remember from your travels through this book? Write down the message. Reflect on how you will carry this message with you into the future.

_____

_____

_____

_____

_____

_____

_____

_____

_____

_____

_____

_____

_____

_____

_____

_____

_____

_____

_____

WELLNESS ❖ ADVICE FROM THE FUTURE. It is a revolutionary idea that you can bend time and visit your past or future selves with your focus and your mind. But this very outcome is available to you at any time in the pages of your journal.

WRITE ON! What advice would your future self offer to keep you motivated and help you to overcome any setbacks or doubts? As you read your answer, underline key phrases. Use them to craft a short, potent mantra that will help you hold onto this advice. Post it where you can see it every day.

_____

_____

_____

_____

_____

YEAR-LONG REVIEW ❖ Consider the entire year of burnout recovery. How do you rank your burnout, compared to where you started? How do you rank your use of these writing processes? How did your intentions manifest? What is different and better?

On a scale of 1 (low) to 7 (high), rate the year.

Burnout?	①	②	③	④	⑤	⑥	⑦
Writing process?	①	②	③	④	⑤	⑥	⑦
Intentions?	①	②	③	④	⑤	⑥	⑦
Noticing changes?	①	②	③	④	⑤	⑥	⑦

WRITE ON! Write observations as you rate your year. Reflect on your overall process.

_____

_____

_____

_____

YOU ❖ THE PROCESS OF RECOVERY ❖ Over 365 days, you have explored your own recovery from the stress, anxiety, fatigue, confusion and depletion of burnout. What have you learned about the recovery process? Some adages from the 12-step movement might be of use: *One day at a time. Take it easy. Feel your feelings. Don't get yourself get too hungry, angry, lonely or tired (HALT).*

WRITE ON! Today, write about your recovery process. Perhaps one of the adages above will serve as your springboard. Or write your own mottos or truth statements about the realizations that have helped you succeed.

_____

_____

_____

_____

_____

_____

GRADUATION ❖ Congratulations! You did it! You have come to the end of this journal, and ideally your burnout recovery has carried you into a new way that predicts future success.

WRITE ON! Today, make yourself a graduation certificate. Make it as dazzling as you'd like. Or make yourself a collage or other piece of art to commemorate your journey. Hang it up somewhere. You've earned it!

_____

_____

_____

_____

_____

_____

ACKNOWLEDGMENTS

KATHLEEN ADAMS: Thanks to Carolyn, Deborah, Leia, Linda, and Nancy for saying yes to this idea, for your expertise, and for a dream collaboration with colleagues who are also friends. Thanks to Sterling Publishing for supporting our multi-voice vision: our editors, Elysia Liang, who wrangled six voices with deft skill, and Barbara Berger; production editor Michael Cea; cover designer Elizabeth Lindy and interior designer Gina Bonnano; and production manager Kevin Iwano. To my clients, students, and trainees, thank you for trusting me as your guide. To my mentor, Dr. Peggy Osna Heller, I am grateful for your wisdom as teacher and friend. To my family, your endless support is soul food. To my husband, Ken Perreault, every writer should be as fortunate as I.

LINDA BARNES: To Kay Adams for inspiring me and inviting me into the widening circle, and to my co-hearts here, I extend blessings. My heartfelt gratitude goes to the students, colleagues, and mentors of the expressive writing community for their loving and generous hearts. I am grateful to the animal teachers who have blessed my life, especially Red Hawk and Mama Bear.

LEIA FRANCISCO: I am grateful to clients who have shared their transition journeys with me, as well as colleagues who have taken transition training into the world. I honor the memory of my mentor, Dr. William Bridges, who created a renaissance in the world of transitions. I honor my co-contributors and, especially, those in burnout as they journal toward renewal.

CAROLYN KOEHNLINE: I want to express thanks to all the journaling pioneers who paved the way, including my wonderful journal therapy mentor, Kay Adams. Deep appreciation goes to all the teachers, colleagues, and clients who helped me find my way to this work. And I extend a special note of gratitude to the amazing women who collaborated on this book and invited me to be a part of it.

DEBORAH ROSS: To my colleagues in this work, I am grateful for your wisdom and generosity and to my students for the privilege of receiving your stories, reflections, and questions. I am grateful to Kay Adams, whose vision of this work and creation of this community is an ongoing gift and blessing. And to my co-hearts in this project, it has been an honor to brainstorm with you to create this offering.

NANCY SCHERLONG: I am grateful to my longtime friend and colleague Kay Adams for her vision and inspiration throughout my journal therapy journey. Her innovation itself is burnout prevention! I am eternally thankful to my husband Larry, who is my heart and soul's support. I thank all my co-contributors, workshop participants, students, and clients for their collaborations. I am honored to have accompanied you on the path to greater health.

SOURCES

TERESA AMABILE, PHD, is a professor at Harvard Business School. Her current research is in how workers manage the transition to retirement. Previously she researched creativity and innovation in the workplace.

SYLVIA BOORSTEIN, PHD, is a psychologist who teaches Buddhism, hatha yoga, and mindfulness meditation for mental and emotional well-being. Her books include *Don't Just Do Something, Sit There.*

BRENÉ BROWN, PHD, is a social science researcher on the themes of courage, vulnerability, and shame. Her best-selling books include *I Thought It Was Just Me (But It Isn't).*

AMANDA CIPRITTO is a certified wellness coach, a certified personal trainer, and a Level 1 CrossFit trainer. She contributes to blogs on health and nutrition.

CORTLAND DAHL, PHD, is a research scientist and chief contemplative officer for the Center for Healthy Minds at the University of Wisconsin-Madison.

RICHARD J. DAVIDSON, PHD, is a psychologist and neuroscientist who created the Center for Healthy Minds at the University of Wisconsin-Madison.

JOHN EVANS, EDD, is an expressive-writing researcher at Duke University and the coauthor of *Expressive Writing: Words that Heal.*

CHARLES FIGLEY, PHD, is the founder of the Tulane Traumatology Institute and the Paul Henry Kurzweg, MD, Distinguished Chair in Disaster Mental Health at Tulane University.

DANIEL GILBERT, PHD, is a psychologist and professor of psychology at Harvard University. He is the author of *Stumbling Toward Happiness* and co-wrote and hosted the NOVA television series, *This Emotional Life.*

MALCOLM GLADWELL is an English-born Canadian journalist, author, and public speaker. He has been a staff writer for *The New Yorker* since 1996. He is the best-selling author of *David and Goliath*, among other books.

DANIEL GOLEMAN, PHD, is a psychologist and former science journalist who authored the best-selling *Emotional Intelligence,* among other books.

RICK HANSON, PHD, is a psychologist and senior fellow at the Greater Good Science Center at University of California, Berkeley. He is the best-selling author of *Buddha's Brain* and *Hardwiring Happiness,* among others.

BILL HETTLER, MD, is a cofounder of the National Wellness Institute, Inc., and its annual conference, both dedicated to whole-person wellness.

JON KABAT-ZINN, PHD, is a psychologist and the founding director of the Stress Reduction Clinic at the University of Massachusetts Medical School. He is the best-selling author of *Wherever You Go, There You Are.*

MATTHEW KILLINGSWORTH, PHD, is a psychologist and creator of a scientific research project to track happiness using a smart phone app. Previously, he worked in the software industry.

JACK KORNFIELD, PHD, is a Buddhist monk who cofounded the Insight Meditation Society in Massachusetts and the Spirit Rock Center in California.

MARSHA LINEHAN, PHD, is a psychologist and creator of dialectical behavior therapy, a treatment model combining mindfulness techniques with cognitive-behavioral theory.

KELLY MCGONIGAL, PHD, is the author of *The Willpower Instinct* and *The Upside of Stress.* She teaches psychology at Stanford University.

AMELIA NAGOSKI, DMA, is a choral conductor who, with her sister Emily, wrote *Burnout: The Secret to Unlocking the Stress Cycle.*

EMILY NAGOSKI, PHD, is a sex educator specializing in the science of women's sexual well-being. With her sister Amelia, she wrote *Burnout: The Secret to Unlocking the Stress Cycle.*

JAMES PENNEBAKER, PHD, is a social science research psychologist who pioneered evidence-based research in expressive writing and health. He is the author of *Writing to Heal,* among others.

ROBERT SAPOLSKY, PHD, is a neuroendocrine researcher and neuroscience professor at Stanford University. He is the author of *Why Zebras Don't Get Ulcers,* among others.

GINA SHAW is a wellness and medical journalist. She has reported for WebMD.com for over 20 years.

DANIEL J. SIEGEL, MD, is a clinical professor of psychiatry at the UCLA School of Medicine and executive director of the Mindsight Institute.

ESTHER M. STERNBERG, MD, is internationally recognized for her discoveries in the science of the mind-body interaction. She is the author of *The Balance Within: The Science Connecting Health and Emotions.*

DAN SULLIVAN is founder and president of The Strategic Coach, Inc., and a coach training program. He is the author of more than thirty publications.

DAN TOMASULO, PHD, is a psychologist in private practice with expertise in positive psychology. He is the author of *Learned Hopefulness,* among others.

DESMOND TUTU, OMSG, CH, GCSTJ, is a South African Anglican cleric and theologian. He is known for his work as an anti-apartheid and human rights activist.

CHRISTINE WILSON-MENDENHALL, PHD, is an associate research scientist for the Center for Healthy Minds at the University of Wisconsin-Madison.

DAN ZIGMOND is a Zen priest ordained in 1998 and has practiced at San Francisco Zen Center and Jikoji Zen Center. He is also a writer and data scientist.

ABOUT THE CONTRIBUTORS

KATHLEEN ADAMS, MA, LPC, PJTR, is a licensed professional counselor and registered poetry/journal therapist who has pioneered the field of expressive writing since 1985. She is the creator of the Center for Journal Therapy; its online professional training division, the Therapeutic Writing Institute; and its online consumer journal writing school, Journalversity. Kathleen is the author of fourteen books, including the best-seller *Journal to the Self*, the textbook *Expressive Writing: Foundations of Practice,* and the first volume in this series, *Journal Therapy for Calming Anxiety.*

LINDA BARNES, MS, teaches poetry, journal writing, and animal wisdom independently and with the Therapeutic Writing Institute and Journalversity. A contributor to Tristine Rainer's classic *The New Diary,* she began her work in 1980 and publishes the Poem of the Week column with writing prompts. She is a past president of the International Federation for Biblio/Poetry Therapy and a practicing poet.

LEIA FRANCISCO, MA, BCC, CJF, CAPF, is a board-certified coach, certified journal facilitator, and certified applied poetry facilitator. As a coach, teacher, and trainer, she specializes in work and life transitions. Leia headed transition teams in both the private and public sectors and pioneered a unique model of using writing as a tool for the transitions process. Her program Writing Through Transitions® and her book *Writing Through Transitions: A Guide for Transforming Life Changes* have been used worldwide. Her greatest joy is helping people find wisdom and strength in their transitions.

CAROLYN KOEHNLINE, MA, LMHC, CJT, is a licensed mental health counselor, a certified journal therapist, and the creator of Gentle Approach Coaching. She specializes in clearing clutter from the home, head, heart, and schedule using journaling processes to access self-kindness, practical guidance, and divine inspiration. Carolyn offers online courses as core faculty of the Therapeutic Writing Institute and Journalversity. She has published three books, including *Confronting Your Clutter* and *Clearing Clutter as a Sacred Act.*

DEBORAH ROSS, MA, LPC, CJT, is a licensed professional counselor and certified journal therapist. She offers private writing instruction and develops expressive writing workshops for the public in healthcare settings and in the meditation community. Retired from private psychotherapy practice, Deborah is a core faculty member at the Therapeutic Writing Institute and Journalversity. She brings her fascination with the neuroscience of well-being and new research in this field to this journal. Deborah is the coauthor with Kathleen Adams of *Your Brain on Ink.*

NANCY SCHERLONG, LCSW, PTR/CJT, CHHC, is a licensed clinical social worker, registered biblio-poetry and journal therapist, and certified holistic health counselor. Her business, Change Your Narrative, is a multi-modal expressive arts coaching, psychotherapy, and training program. Nancy is currently president of the International Federation for Biblio-Poetry Therapy as well as a core faculty member of the Therapeutic Writing Institute, Kint Institute, Adelphi University, and Columbia University. She is a contributor to several publications on poetry and therapeutic writing.